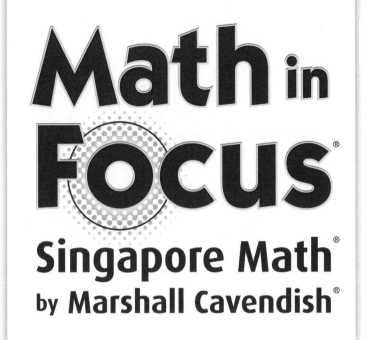

GRADE
2B

Workbook

Consultant and Author
Dr. Fong Ho Kheong

Authors
Chelvi Ramakrishnan and Michelle Choo

U.S. Consultants
Dr. Richard Bisk
Andy Clark
Patsy F. Kanter

Marshall Cavendish
Education

U.S. Distributor

**Houghton
Mifflin
Harcourt**

© 2018 Marshall Cavendish Education Pte Ltd

Published by Marshall Cavendish Education
Times Centre, 1 New Industrial Road, Singapore 536196
Customer Service Hotline: (65) 6213 9688
US Office Tel: (1-914) 332 8888 | Fax: (1-914) 332 8882
E-mail: cs@mceducation.com
Website: www.mceducation.com

Distributed by
Houghton Mifflin Harcourt
222 Berkeley Street
Boston, MA 02116
Tel: 617-351-5000
Website: www.hmheducation.com/mathinfocus

Cover: © Tetra Images/Getty Images, © PictureNet/Spirit/Corbis.
Images provided by Houghton Mifflin Harcourt.

First published 2018

ISBN 978-1-328-88108-3

Printed in Singapore

7 8 9   1401   23 22 21 20
4500814554   A B C D E

Contents

Mental Math and Estimation

Practice 1   Meaning of Sum   1
Practice 2   Mental Addition   3
Practice 3   Meaning of Difference   7
Practice 4   Mental Subtraction   11
Practice 5   Rounding Numbers to Estimate   15

Chapter Review/Test   21

Money

Practice 1   Coins and Bills   23
Practice 2   Comparing Amounts of Money   35
Practice 3   Real-World Problems: Money   39

Math Journal   42
Put on Your Thinking Cap! Challenging Practice 43
Put on Your Thinking Cap! Problem Solving   44
Chapter Review/Test   45

CHAPTER 12 Fractions

Practice 1	Understanding Fractions	47
Practice 2	Comparing Fractions	53
Practice 3	Adding and Subtracting Like Fractions	55

Put on Your Thinking Cap! Challenging Practice — 60
Chapter Review/Test — 61

Cumulative Review for Chapters 10 to 12 — 65

CHAPTER 13 Customary Measurement of Length

Practice 1	Measuring in Feet	75
Practice 2	Comparing Lengths in Feet	79
Practice 3	Measuring in Inches	81
Practice 4	Comparing Lengths in Inches and Feet	85
Practice 5	Real-World Problems: Customary Length	89

Put on Your Thinking Cap! Challenging Practice — 93
Put on Your Thinking Cap! Problem Solving — 94
Chapter Review/Test — 95

CHAPTER 14 Time

Practice 1	The Minute Hand	99
Practice 2	Reading and Writing Time	103
Practice 3	Using A.M. and P.M.	109
Practice 4	Elapsed Time	113

Math Journal	120
Put on Your Thinking Cap! Challenging Practice	121
Put on Your Thinking Cap! Problem Solving	122
Chapter Review/Test	123

Cumulative Review for Chapters 13 and 14   125

CHAPTER 15 Multiplication Tables of 3 and 4

Practice 1	Multiplying 3: Skip-Counting	135
Practice 2	Multiplying 3: Using Dot Paper	137

Math Journal	142

Practice 3	Multiplying 4: Skip-Counting	143
Practice 4	Multiplying 4: Using Dot Paper	145
Practice 5	Divide Using Related Multiplication Facts	149

Put on Your Thinking Cap! Challenging Practice	153
Put on Your Thinking Cap! Problem Solving	154
Chapter Review/Test	155

v

Using Bar Models: Multiplication and Division

Practice 1	Real-World Problems: Multiplication	157
Math Journal		162
Practice 2	Real-World Problems: Division	163
Practice 3	Real-World Problems: Measurement and Money	167
Put on Your Thinking Cap! Challenging Practice		175
Put on Your Thinking Cap! Problem Solving		176
Chapter Review/Test		177

Graphs and Line Plots

Practice 1	Reading Picture Graphs with Scales	181
Practice 2	Making Picture Graphs	185
Practice 3	Real-World Problems: Picture Graphs	193
Practice 4	Bar Graphs and Line Plots	197
Put on Your Thinking Cap! Challenging Practice		199
Put on Your Thinking Cap! Problem Solving		200
Chapter Review/Test		201

Cumulative Review for Chapters 15 to 17   207

Lines and Surfaces

Practice 1   Parts of Lines and Curves   215

Math Journal   220
Practice 2   Flat and Curved Surfaces   221

Put on Your Thinking Cap! Challenging Practice   227
Chapter Review/Test   229

Shapes and Patterns

Practice 1   Plane Shapes   231
Practice 2   Solid Shapes   243
Practice 3   Making Patterns   245

Math Journal   249
Put on Your Thinking Cap! Challenging Practice   250
Chapter Review/Test   251

Cumulative Review for Chapters 18 and 19   255

End-of-Year Review   259

CHAPTER 10 Mental Math and Estimation

Practice 1 Meaning of Sum

Find the sum of the numbers.

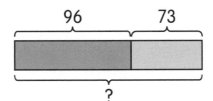
1.   700 and 200

```
    7 0 0
  + 2 0 0
  ┌─────┐
  │     │
  └─────┘
```

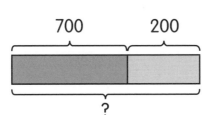

The sum of _____ and _____ is _____.

2.   215 and 507

```
    2 1 5
  + 5 0 7
  ┌─────┐
  │     │
  └─────┘
```

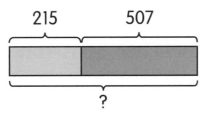

The sum of _____ and _____ is _____.

Solve.
Use bar models to help you.

3.   Al spent $27 on a shirt and $120 on books.
   Find the sum of money Al spent.

   _____ + _____ = _____

   The sum of money Al spent is $_____.

4.   Harry is 12 years old.
   His sister is 9 years younger.
   Find the sum of their ages.

   _____ – _____ = _____

   _____ + _____ = _____

   The sum of their ages is _____ years.

5.   Greg has collected 32 green jumping beans.
   His mother gives him 15 red jumping beans more.
   Find the sum of jumping beans Greg has now.

   _____ + _____ = _____

   The sum of jumping beans Greg has now is _____.

Practice 2   Mental Addition

Climb each step by adding mentally.

1.

Find the missing numbers.
Add mentally.

┌─ **Example** ─────────────┐

38 + 7 = ?

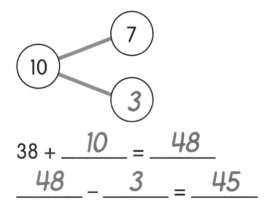

38 + ___10___ = ___48___

___48___ − ___3___ = ___45___

So, 38 + 7 = ___45___.

└──────────────────────────┘

2.   75 + 6 = ?

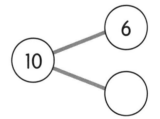

75 + _____ = _____

_____ − _____ = _____

So, 75 + 6 = _____.

3.   69 + 5 = _____

4.   48 + 4 = _____

5.   29 + 9 = _____

6.   65 + 8 = _____

Find the missing numbers.
Add mentally.

Example

123 + 5 = ?

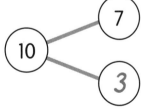

$$\underline{\quad 3 \quad} + 5 = \underline{\quad 8 \quad}$$

$$\underline{\quad 120 \quad} + \underline{\quad 8 \quad} = \underline{\quad 128 \quad}$$

So, 123 + 5 = $\underline{\quad 128 \quad}$.

7. 632 + 7 = _____

8. 712 + 3 = _____

9. 534 + 5 = _____

Example

409 + 7 = ?

7

10

3

409 + $\underline{\quad 10 \quad}$ = $\underline{\quad 419 \quad}$

$\underline{\quad 419 \quad}$ − $\underline{\quad 3 \quad}$ = $\underline{\quad 416 \quad}$

So, 409 + 7 = $\underline{\quad 416 \quad}$.

10. 375 + 6 = _____

11. 275 + 8 = _____

12. 629 + 9 = _____

Find the missing numbers.
Add mentally.

Example

$246 + 20 = ?$

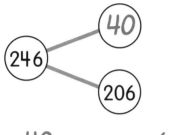

$\underline{\quad 40 \quad} + 20 = \underline{\quad 60 \quad}$

$\underline{\quad 206 \quad} + \underline{\quad 60 \quad} = \underline{\quad 266 \quad}$

So, $246 + 20 = \underline{\quad 266 \quad}$.

13. $348 + 50 = \underline{\hspace{2cm}}$

14. $741 + 30 = \underline{\hspace{2cm}}$

15. $653 + 10 = \underline{\hspace{2cm}}$

Example

$352 + 70 = ?$

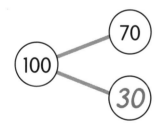

$352 + \underline{\quad 100 \quad} = \underline{\quad 452 \quad}$

$\underline{\quad 452 \quad} - \underline{\quad 30 \quad} = \underline{\quad 422 \quad}$

So, $352 + 70 = \underline{\quad 422 \quad}$.

16. $427 + 80 = \underline{\hspace{2cm}}$

17. $535 + 90 = \underline{\hspace{2cm}}$

18. $164 + 60 = \underline{\hspace{2cm}}$

Find the missing numbers.
Add mentally.

Example

$315 + 200 = ?$

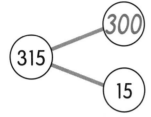

$\underline{\quad 300 \quad} + 200 = \underline{\quad 500 \quad}$

$\underline{\quad 15 \quad} + \underline{\quad 500 \quad} = \underline{\quad 515 \quad}$

So, $315 + 200 = \underline{\quad 515 \quad}$.

19. $765 + 100 = ?$

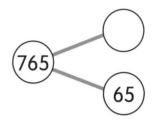

$\underline{\qquad} + 100 = \underline{\qquad}$

$\underline{\qquad} + \underline{\qquad} = \underline{\qquad}$

So, $765 + 100 = \underline{\qquad}$.

Add mentally.

20. $452 + 500 = \underline{\qquad}$

21. $264 + 300 = \underline{\qquad}$

22. $412 + 300 = \underline{\qquad}$

23. $178 + 300 = \underline{\qquad}$

24. $708 + 200 = \underline{\qquad}$

25. $320 + 600 = \underline{\qquad}$

Practice 3   Meaning of Difference

Find the difference between the numbers.

┌─ **Example** ───┐

40 and 17

$$\begin{array}{r} 4\ 0 \\ -\ 1\ 7 \\ \hline \end{array}$$

__*40*__ − __*17*__ = __*23*__

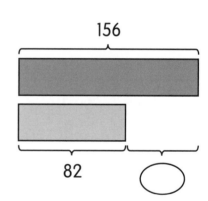

40

17   ⟨*23*⟩

The difference between 40 and 17 is __*23*__.

└───┘

1.   156 and 82

$$\begin{array}{r} 1\ 5\ 6 \\ -\ \ \ 8\ 2 \\ \hline \end{array}$$

_____ − _____ = _____

156

82   ◯

The difference between 156 and 82 is _____.

2.   800 and 785

$$\begin{array}{r} 8\ 0\ 0 \\ -\ 7\ 8\ 5 \\ \hline \end{array}$$

_____ − _____ = _____

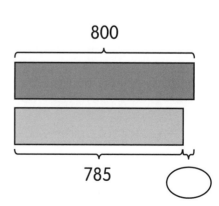

800

785   ◯

The difference between 800 and 785 is _____.

Solve.
Use bar models to help you.

3. Tonya collected 320 friendship bracelets and her sister collected 290.
Find the difference between the number of friendship bracelets.

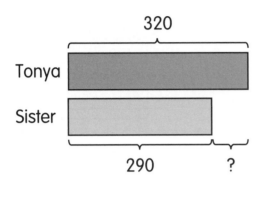

_____ − _____ = _____

The difference is _____ friendship bracelets.

4. Joe and Susan went for a run.
Joe ran 24 laps and Susan ran 15 laps.
Find the difference between the number of laps they ran.

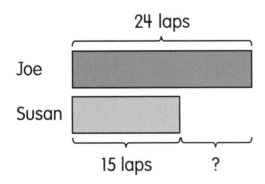

_____ − _____ = _____

The difference is _____ laps.

Solve.
Use bar models to help you.

5. Kiki baked 120 muffins on Monday.
She baked 219 muffins on Tuesday.
What is the difference between these two amounts?

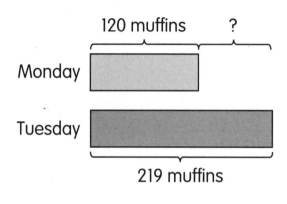

_____ − _____ = _____

The difference is _____ muffins.

6. Mr. Wong wants to buy a camera that costs $401.
He saved $315.
What is the difference between the amounts of money?

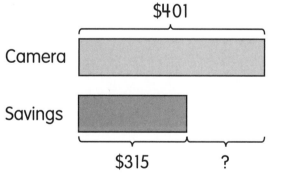

The difference shows how much more money Mr. Wong needs to buy the camera.

_____ − _____ = _____

The difference is $ _____.

Solve.
Use bar models to help you.

7.　Elizabeth has a blue ribbon and a red ribbon.
　　The blue ribbon is 27 centimeters long.
　　The red ribbon is 18 centimeters long.
　　What is the difference between their lengths?

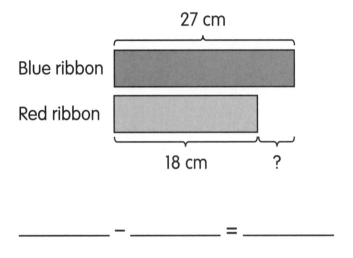

_____ – _____ = _____

The difference is _____ centimeters.

Practice 4   Mental Subtraction

Find the missing numbers.
Subtract mentally.

Example

43 – 6 = ?

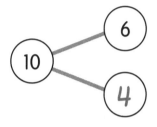

43 – ___10___ = ___33___

___33___ + ___4___ = ___37___

So, 43 – 6 = ___37___.

1.   56 – 8 = ?

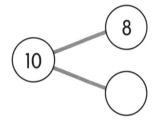

56 – _____ = _____

_____ + _____ = _____

So, 56 – 8 = _____.

Subtract mentally.

2.   84 – 7 = _____

3.   38 – 9 = _____

4.   62 – 8 = _____

5.   76 – 7 = _____

Find the missing numbers.
Subtract mentally.

> **Example**
>
> 789 − 5 = ?
>
>
> 789 → 9
> 789 → 780
>
> ___9___ − 5 = ___4___
>
> ___780___ + ___4___ = ___784___
>
> So, 789 − 5 = ___784___.

6. 398 − 4 = _____

7. 427 − 2 = _____

8. 358 − 6 = _____

Find the missing numbers.
Subtract mentally.

> **Example**
>
> 364 − 6 = ?
>
>
> 10 → 6
> 10 → 4
>
> 364 − ___10___ = ___354___
>
> ___354___ + ___4___ = ___358___
>
> So, 364 − 6 = ___358___.

9. 472 − 3 = _____

10. 513 − 9 = _____

11. 394 − 7 = _____

Find the missing numbers.
Subtract mentally.

Example

$348 - 20 = ?$

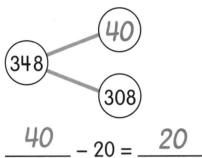

$\underline{\quad 40 \quad} - 20 = \underline{\quad 20 \quad}$

$\underline{\quad 308 \quad} + \underline{\quad 20 \quad} = \underline{\quad 328 \quad}$

So, $348 - 20 = \underline{\quad 328 \quad}$.

12. $475 - 40 = $ _____

13. $466 - 30 = $ _____

14. $654 - 50 = $ _____

Find the missing numbers.
Subtract mentally.

Example

$641 - 50 = ?$

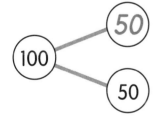

$641 - \underline{\quad 100 \quad} = \underline{\quad 541 \quad}$

$\underline{\quad 541 \quad} + \underline{\quad 50 \quad} = \underline{\quad 591 \quad}$

So, $641 - 50 = \underline{\quad 591 \quad}$.

15. $516 - 70 = $ _____

16. $228 - 30 = $ _____

17. $436 - 40 = $ _____

Find the missing numbers.
Subtract mentally.

```
┌─────────── Example ──────────────┐
│                                  │
│   256 − 100 = ?                  │
│                                  │
```

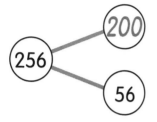

$$\underline{\quad 200 \quad} - 100 = \underline{\quad 100 \quad}$$

$$\underline{\quad 56 \quad} + \underline{\quad 100 \quad} = \underline{\quad 156 \quad}$$

So, 256 − 100 = $\underline{\quad 156 \quad}$.

18.   832 − 400 = ?

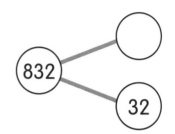

$$\underline{\qquad} - 400 = \underline{\qquad}$$

$$\underline{\qquad} + \underline{\qquad} = \underline{\qquad}$$

So, 832 − 400 = $\underline{\qquad}$.

Find the missing numbers.
Subtract mentally.

19.   348 − 300 = $\underline{\qquad}$

20.   548 − 300 = $\underline{\qquad}$

21.   615 − 400 = $\underline{\qquad}$

22.   465 − 200 = $\underline{\qquad}$

Practice 5   Rounding Numbers to Estimate

Mark each number with an X on the number line.

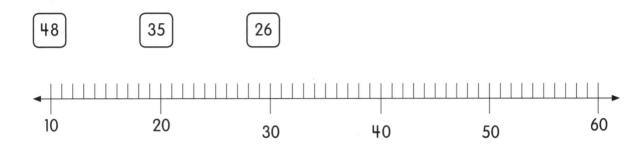

Round each number to the nearest ten.
Circle it on the number line. Then fill in the blanks.

Example

12 is nearer to ___*10*___ than to ___*20*___.

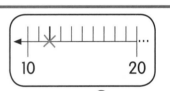

12 is about ___*10*___ when rounded to the nearest ten.

1.   48 is nearer to _____ than to _____.

48 is about _____ when rounded to the nearest ten.

2.   35 is about _____ when rounded to the nearest ten.

3.   26 is nearer to _____ than to _____.

26 is about _____ when rounded to the nearest ten.

Look at the digits in the tens place. Then fill in the blanks.

Example

37 is between ___30___ and ___40___.

---

4.   86   86 is between _____ and _____.

5.   93   93 is between _____ and _____.

6.   286   286 is between _____ and _____.

7.   721   721 is between _____ and _____.

Mark each number with an X on the number line.
Round each number to the nearest ten.
Circle the number on the number line.
Then fill in the last column of the table.

Number	Number line	Write using 'is about'
Example 315	310 315 (320)	*315* is about *320*.
8. 769	760 770	
9. 501	500 510	
10. 896	890 900	

Name: _____   Date: _____

Complete the table.

	Number	Rounded to the nearest ten	Write using 'is about'
	Example 78	80	78 is about 80
11.	15		
12.	34		
13.	217		
14.	697		
15.	728		

**The numbers in each problem are rounded to the nearest ten.
Find the greatest and least number that is rounded.
Use the number line to help you.**

Example

Mr. Johnson spent about $80 at a department store.

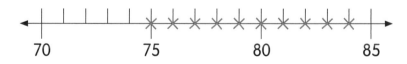

70   75   80   85

The greatest amount he could have spent is $____84____.

The least amount he could have spent is $____75____.

16. Charles drinks about 790 milliliters of fruit juice in one day.

The greatest amount he could have had is _____ milliliters.

The least amount he could have had is _____ milliliters.

17. Shateel ran about 750 meters.

The greatest distance she could have run is _____ meters.

The least distance she could have run is _____ meters.

18. The mass of a bag of potatoes is about 830 grams.

The greatest mass of the potatoes could be _____ grams.

The least mass of the potatoes could be _____ grams.

Find the sum or difference.
Then round each number to the nearest ten.
Estimate the sum or difference to check that the answers
are reasonable.

Example

763 + 36 = 799

763 is about ___*760*___.

36 is about ___*40*___.

760 + 40 = ___*800*___.

So, 763 + 36 is about ___*800*___.

Is the answer reasonable?

Explain. ___*Yes, because 800 is close to 799.*___

19. 238 + 98 = _____

238 is about _____.

98 is about _____.

_____ + _____ = _____.

So, 238 + 98 is about _____.

Is the answer reasonable? Explain. _____

20. 847 – 95 = _____

847 is about _____.

95 is about _____.

_____ – _____ = _____.

So, 846 – 95 is about _____.

Is the answer reasonable? Explain. _____

21. $781 + 49 =$ _____

Check: _____ + _____ = _____.

Is the answer reasonable? Explain. _____

_____

_____

22. $259 - 72 =$ _____

Check: _____ − _____ = _____.

Is the answer reasonable? Explain. _____

_____

23. The school principal has $900 to buy items for the school.
Round the cost of each item to the nearest ten.
Then estimate the total cost.

A set of 4 textbooks costs $96.

a. 96 is _____ when rounded to the nearest ten.

A printer costs $215.

b. 215 is _____ when rounded to the nearest ten.

A camera costs $147.

c. 147 is _____ when rounded to the nearest ten.

A computer costs $385.

d. 385 is _____ when rounded to the nearest ten.

The estimated total cost is $_____.

Does the principal have enough money to pay for all the items?

_____

Chapter Review/Test

Vocabulary

Fill in the blanks with words from the box.

sum
difference
nearest ten
reasonable

1. You can use an estimate to check that a sum

   is _____.

2. 86 is 90 when rounded to the _____.

3. Add to find the _____ of two or more numbers.

4. Subtract to find the _____ between two or more numbers.

Concepts and Skills
Add mentally.

5. $325 + 9 =$ _____

6. $436 + 20 =$ _____

7. $691 + 70 =$ _____

8. $635 + 300 =$ _____

Subtract mentally.

9. $541 - 5 =$ _____

10. $863 - 50 =$ _____

11. $238 - 70 =$ _____

12. $617 - 400 =$ _____

Round each number to the nearest ten.

13. 65 is about _____.

14. 132 is about _____.

15. 29 is about _____.

16. 396 is about _____.

**Find the sum or difference. Then round each number
to the nearest ten to check that the answers are reasonable.**

17. 76 + 83 = _____

_____ + _____ = _____

18. 182 + 95 = _____

_____ + _____ = _____

19. 628 − 145 = _____

_____ − _____ = _____

20. 598 − 136 = _____

_____ − _____ = _____

Problem Solving

Solve. Then use estimation to check that the answers are reasonable.

21. Mrs. Brown buys a set of books and a giant teddy bear.
The set of books costs $154.
The giant teddy bear costs $122.
Find the sum of the amount for both prices.

_____ + _____ = _____

Check: _____ + _____ = _____.

Is the answer reasonable? Explain. _____

_____

The two things cost about $_____.

22. Pete earns $103 a month delivering newspapers.
Shawn earns $175 a month delivering pizzas.
What is the difference in the amounts they earn?

_____ − _____ = _____

Check: _____ − _____ = _____.

Is the answer reasonable? Explain. _____

_____

The difference is about $_____.

CHAPTER 11 Money

Practice 1   Coins and Bills

Circle the bills that make the given amount.

Example

1.

 =

2.

 =

Circle the coins that make one dollar.

3.

 =

4.

 =

Find the value of the coins.
Then write *less than, equal to,* or *more than.*

Example

_____more than_____ $1.

5.

_____ $1.

6.

_____ $1.

7.

_____ $1.

Write the amount of money.

┌─ **Example** ───┐

$10

└──┘

8.

$_____

9.

$_____

Write the amount of money.

Example

Eighty-two dollars and seven cents

$ *82.07*

10.

Ninety-six cents

$_____

11.

Sixty-one dollars

$_____

Write the amount of money.

12.

Fourteen dollars and ninety-nine cents

$_____

13.

Thirty dollars and fifty cents

$_____

14.

Fifteen dollars

$_____

15.

Seventy-eight dollars and twenty-five cents

$_____

Fill in the blanks.

Example

$20.00 • • • • • • • • • • • • • • • • ____20____ dollars ____0____ cents

16. $.03 • • • • • • • • • • • • • • • _____ dollars _____ cents

17. $40.20 • • • • • • • • • • • • • • • • _____ dollars _____ cents

18. $27.15 • • • • • • • • • • • • • • • • _____ dollars _____ cents

Match.

19.

 • • $1.45

20.

 • • $.15

21.

 • • $8.00

22.

 • • $13.35

Name: _____ Date: _____

Count the money.
Then circle the correct amount.

Example

$ 2.06

$20.60

$26

23.

$7.00

$7.07

$7.70

24.

$1.10

$11.00

$.11

25.

$50.15

$.65

$5.15

Complete.

_____6_____ dollars

and ___10___ cents or

$___6.10___

26.

_____ dollars

and _____ cents or

$_____

27.

_____ dollars

and _____ cents or

$_____

28.

_____ dollars

and _____ cents or

$_____

29.

_____ dollar

and _____ cents or

$_____

30.

_____ dollar

and _____ cents or

$_____

Write the amount of money in two ways.

┌─ **Example** ──┐

_____65_____ ¢ or $____.65____

31.

_____ ¢ or $_____

32.

$_____ or $_____

33.

$_____ or $_____

Write the amount of money in two ways.

Example

$ _____2.20_____ or _____220_____ ¢

34.

$_____ or _____ ¢

35.

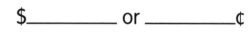

$_____ or _____ ¢

36.

$_____ or _____ ¢

Write the cents in dollars and cents.

20¢   _$.20_

37. 120¢   _____

38. 543¢   _____

39. 106¢   _____

40. 350¢   _____

41. 83¢   _____

42. 17¢   _____

43. 2¢   _____

Write the dollars and cents in cents.

Example

$4.80   _480¢_

44. $3.51   _____

45. $6.95   _____

46. $1.05   _____

47. $.44   _____

48. $.69   _____

49. $8   _____

50. $7   _____

Practice 2   Comparing Amounts of Money

Compare the amounts.
Complete the tables and fill in the blanks.

Example

Joey
$14.20

Dollars	Cents
14	20

Carl
$15.00

Dollars	Cents
15	00

First, compare
the dollars. 15 is
greater than 14.

$_*15.00*_ is more than $_*14.20*_.

$_*14.20*_ is less than $_*15.00*_.

1.

Mae
$70.40

Dollars	Cents

Karen
$70.35

Dollars	Cents

$_____ > $_____

$_____ < $_____

2.

Dollars	Cents

$16.70

Dollars	Cents

$16.15

Dollars	Cents

$16.45

Are all of these amounts the same? _____

$_____ is the greatest amount.

$_____ is the least amount.

3.

Dollars	Cents

$45.30

Dollars	Cents

$42.95

Dollars	Cents

$45.75

Which is the greatest amount? _____

Which is the least amount? _____

Name: _____   Date: _____

Write the amount in each set.
Then check (✓) the set that has the greater value.

Example

$50.00

$51.00   ✓

4.

_____

_____

5.

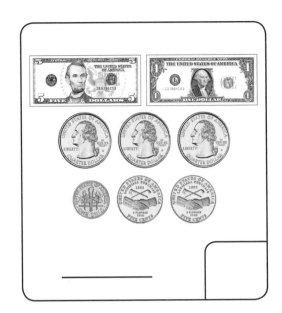

Circle the amount that is less.

6. $3.85 $4.10

7. $62.40 $62.25

Circle the amount that is more.

8. $28.90 $27.95

9. $71.09 $7.90

Compare the amounts.

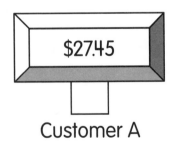

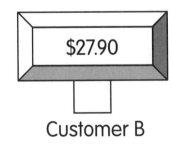

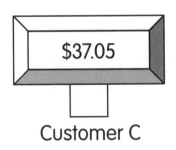

Customer A   Customer B   Customer C

10.   Which customer paid the most? Customer _____

11.   Which customer paid the least? Customer _____

Practice 3   Real-World Problems: Money

Solve.

Draw bar models to help you.

1.   Maddy buys a pencil for 25¢ and an eraser for 17¢.
She gives the cashier 50¢.
How much change does she get?

2.   The Lesters have $600.
They spent $110 on food and $97 on electricity.
How much do they have left?

3.   Walter buys a notebook for 50¢.
He buys another notebook that costs 12¢ more.
How much does Walter pay in all?

Solve.
Write your answers using $ or ¢.

95¢

80¢

65¢

$1

4. Tyler buys a book and a pen.
    How much does he spend?

5. Rosie buys a teddy bear.
    Pamela buys a pencil sharpener.
    How much do they spend?

6. How much more is a pen than a pencil sharpener?

7. Jessie has a dollar bill and a quarter.
She wants to buy a teddy bear and a book.

    a. Does she have enough money?

    b. If not, how much more does she need?

8. Henry has a $10 bill.
He buys a teddy bear, a book, and a pen.
How much does he have left?

Math Journal

Shawn made some mistakes in his homework.
Help him correct the mistakes.

Example

Shawn's mistake: 35¢ = ___*$3.50*___

Correct answer: ___*35¢ = $.35*___

1. Shawn's mistake: One dollar and sixty cents = $1.06

Correct answer: _____

2. Shawn's mistake: 450¢ = $450

Correct answer: _____

3. Shawn's mistake: $6 is $5 less than $10.

Correct answer: _____

4. Shawn's mistake: $90 is $10 more than $100.

Correct answer: _____

Put On Your Thinking Cap!

Challenging Practice

Draw the amount of money using $5¢$, $10¢$, $25¢$, $1, and $5.

Example

$5.70

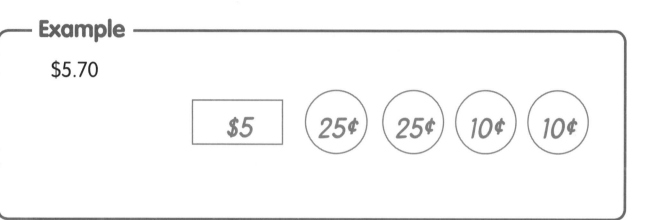

$5   25¢   25¢   10¢   10¢

1. $4.60

2. $9.40

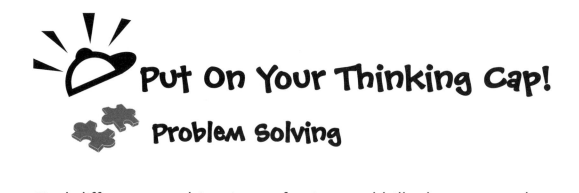

Put On Your Thinking Cap!

Problem Solving

Find different combinations of coins and bills that can make each amount.

Example

$8.50

	$20	$10	$5	$1	25¢	10¢
Set A			1	3	2	
Set B			1	2	6	
Set C			1	3		5

1. $60.30

	$20	$10	$5	$1	25¢	10¢
Set A						
Set B						
Set C						

2. $25.00

	$20	$10	$5	$1	25¢	10¢
Set A						
Set B						
Set C						

Which amount is the greatest? _____

Chapter Review/Test

Vocabulary

$
\begin{array}{|l|}
\hline
\$ \rule{2cm}{0.4pt} \\
\text{¢} \rule{2cm}{0.4pt} \\
\text{decimal point} \\
\hline
\end{array}
$

Fill in the blanks with words or symbols from the box.

1. A _____ separates the dollars from the cents.

2. 100¢ makes _____ 1.

3. $.75 can also be written as 75 _____.

Concepts and Skills

Identify the value of each bill or coin.

4.   **5.**   **6.**  **7.**

_____   _____   _____   _____

Write the amount of money in words and numbers.

8.

_____ or _____¢

9.

_____ or _____¢

Write the amount in dollars or cents.

10. 50¢ = $_____

11. 125¢ = $_____

12. $16 = _____¢

13. $7.02 = _____¢

Compare.

$71.25 $72.52 $17.95

14. Which is the least amount? _____

15. Which is the greatest amount? _____

Problem Solving

Solve. Draw bar models to help you.

16. Jeffrey has two $1 bills.
He buys an ice cream for 70¢.
How much does he have left?

He has _____ left.

17. Anita has $150.
She spends $53 on books and $35 on a pair of shoes.
How much does she have left?

She has $_____ left.

Name: _____   Date: _____

Fractions

Practice 1   Understanding Fractions

Put an *X* in the box if the shape is divided into equal parts.

Example

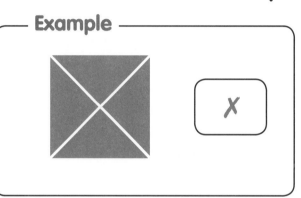

1.

2.

3.

4.

5.

6.

7.
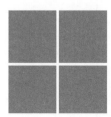

Look at the pictures.
Then fill in the blanks.

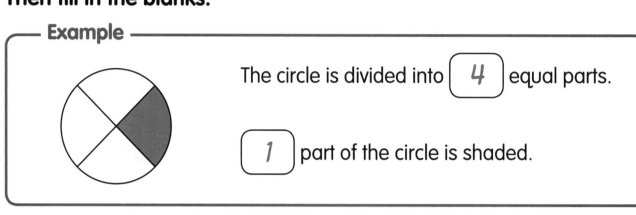

The circle is divided into ⌈ 4 ⌉ equal parts.

⌈ 1 ⌉ part of the circle is shaded.

8.

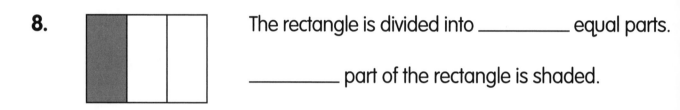

The rectangle is divided into _____ equal parts.

_____ part of the rectangle is shaded.

Circle the fraction and words that match the picture.

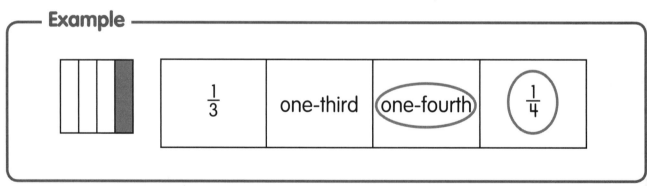

| $\frac{1}{3}$ | one-third | (one-fourth) | ($\frac{1}{4}$) |

9.

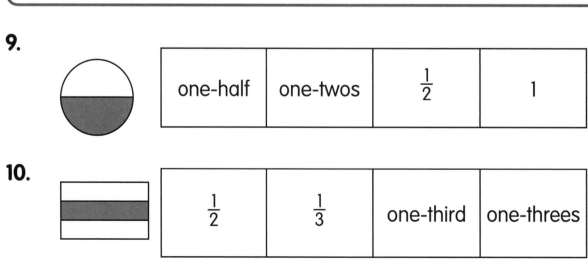

| one-half | one-twos | $\frac{1}{2}$ | 1 |

10.

| $\frac{1}{2}$ | $\frac{1}{3}$ | one-third | one-threes |

Mark with an ✗ the fractional part that does not belong in each row.

Example

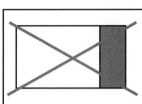 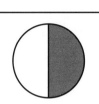 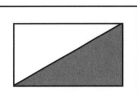   one-half

11.

one-fourth 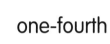 ...

12.

   one-third

Fill in the blanks.

Example

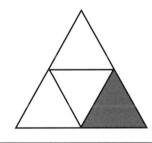

_____1_____ out of _____4_____ equal parts is shaded.

$\frac{1}{4}$

_____ of the figure is shaded.

13.

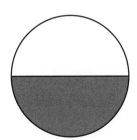

_____ out of _____ equal parts is shaded.

_____ of the figure is shaded.

14.

_____ out of _____ equal parts is shaded.

_____ of the figure is shaded.

15.

_____ out of _____ equal parts is shaded.

_____ of the figure is shaded.

Write a fraction for each shaded part.

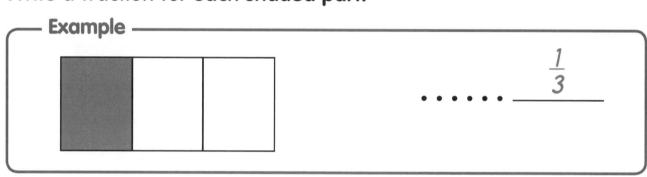

Example

$\cdots\cdots$ $\dfrac{1}{3}$

16.

$\cdots\cdots$ _____

17.

$\cdots\cdots$ _____

18.

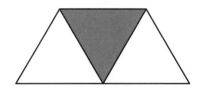

• • • • • • _____

19.

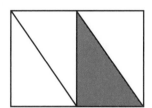

• • • • • • _____

Shade part(s) of each figure to show the fraction.

20. $\frac{1}{3}$

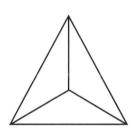

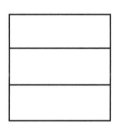

21. $\frac{1}{4}$

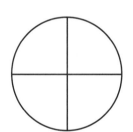

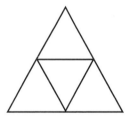

22. $\frac{1}{2}$

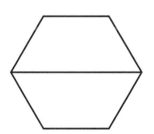

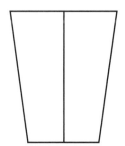

Match the words and fractions to the figures.

23.

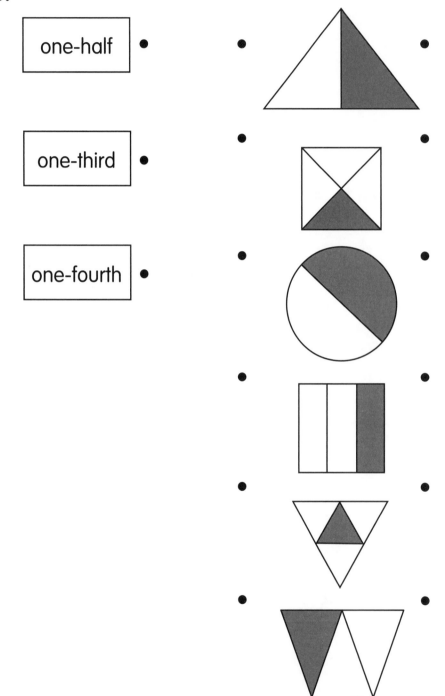

one-half •

one-third •

one-fourth •

$\frac{1}{4}$

$\frac{1}{2}$

$\frac{1}{3}$

Practice 2   Comparing Fractions

Write the fraction of the shaded part or parts.
Then compare the fractions.

Example

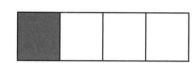

$\dfrac{1}{4}$

_____ is shaded.

$\dfrac{1}{3}$

_____ is shaded.

$\dfrac{1}{3}$

_____ is greater than ___$\dfrac{1}{4}$___.

$\dfrac{1}{4}$

_____ is less than ___$\dfrac{1}{3}$___.

1.

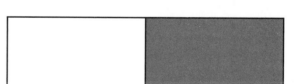

_____ is shaded.   _____ is shaded.

_____ is greater than _____.

_____ is less than _____.

Compare.
Write > or < in ⬡.

2.

$\frac{1}{2}$ is shaded.

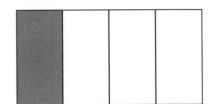

$\frac{1}{4}$ is shaded.

$\frac{1}{4} \bigcirc \frac{1}{2}$

$\frac{1}{2} \bigcirc \frac{1}{4}$

Write a fraction for each shaded part.
Then arrange the fractions from the greatest to least.

3. 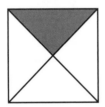   4. 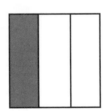   5.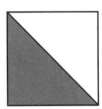

_____   _____   _____

_____

greatest   least

Practice 3 Adding and Subtracting Like Fractions

Write the fraction for the shaded parts.

1.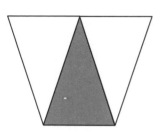

2.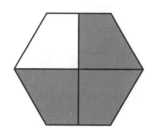

3.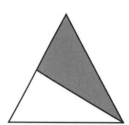

_____

_____

_____

Shade the parts to show the sum.

— **Example** —

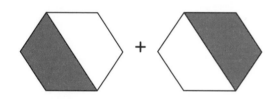

4.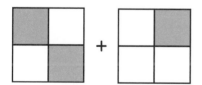

5.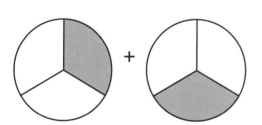

Shade the parts to show the sum.

6.

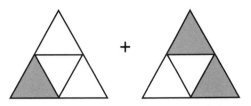 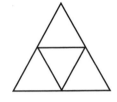

7.

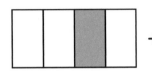 +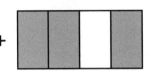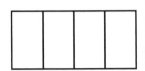

Add.
Use models to help you.

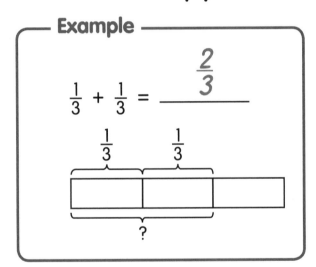

Example

$\frac{1}{3} + \frac{1}{3} =$ _____ $\frac{2}{3}$

$\frac{1}{3}$ $\frac{1}{3}$

?

8. $\frac{1}{4} + \frac{2}{4} =$ _____

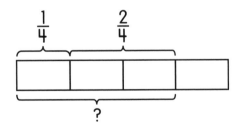

$\frac{1}{4}$ $\frac{2}{4}$

?

Add.
Use models to help you.

9. $\frac{1}{2} + \frac{1}{2} =$ _____

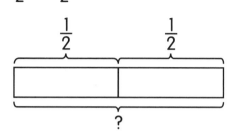

10. $\frac{1}{3} +$ _____ $= 1$

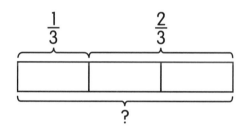

Shade the parts to show the difference.

┌─ **Example** ─────────────────────────────────┐

└───┘

11.

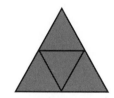 

12.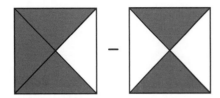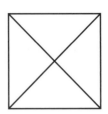

13.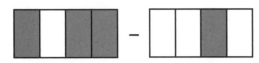

14.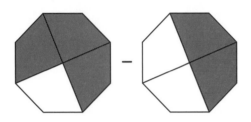

Subtract.
Use models to help you.

Example

$$1 - \frac{2}{3} = \underline{\quad \frac{1}{3} \quad}$$

15. $\frac{3}{4} - \frac{1}{4} = \underline{\hspace{3cm}}$

Subtract.
Use models to help you.

16. $\frac{2}{3} - \frac{1}{3} =$ _____

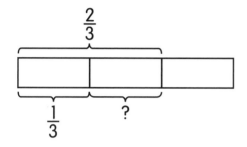

17. $1 -$ _____ $= \frac{1}{4}$

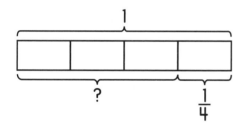

18. $\frac{3}{4} - \frac{2}{4} =$ _____

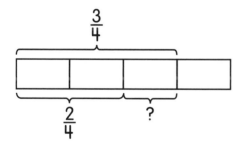

Put On Your Thinking Cap!

Challenging Practice

1. _____ more parts need to be shaded to show $\frac{3}{4}$.

2. _____ more part needs to be shaded to show $\frac{2}{3}$.

3. _____ more parts need to be shaded to show $\frac{4}{4}$.

Chapter Review/Test

Vocabulary

Fill in the blanks with words from the box.

whole
equal
greater than
less than

1.

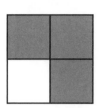

$\frac{3}{4}$ means 3 out of 4 _____ parts.

2.

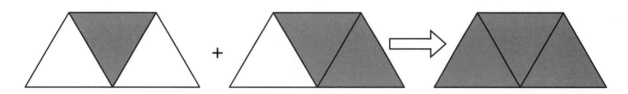

$\frac{1}{3}$ and $\frac{2}{3}$ make a _____.

3.

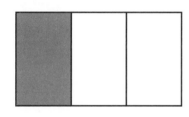

$\frac{1}{3}$ $\frac{1}{2}$

$\frac{1}{3}$ is _____ $\frac{1}{2}$.

4.

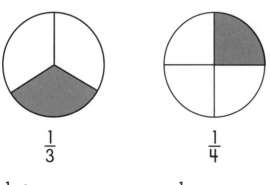

$\frac{1}{3}$ $\frac{1}{4}$

$\frac{1}{3}$ is _____ $\frac{1}{4}$.

Concepts and Skills

5. **Match.**

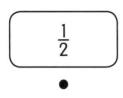

$\frac{1}{2}$ •

$\frac{1}{4}$ •

$\frac{1}{3}$ •

•

•

•

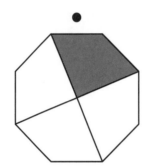

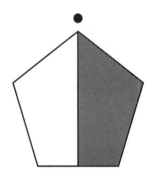

Write > or < in ◯.

6. $\frac{1}{2}$

$\frac{1}{3}$

$\frac{1}{2}$ ◯ $\frac{1}{3}$

7. $\frac{1}{4}$

$\frac{1}{2}$

$\frac{1}{4}$ ◯ $\frac{1}{2}$

Name: _____   **Date:** _____

Write > or < in ◯.

8. $\frac{1}{3}$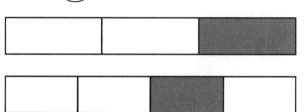

$\frac{1}{4}$

$\frac{1}{3}$ ◯ $\frac{1}{4}$

9. Now arrange the fractions in order from least to greatest.

◻ ◻ ◻

10. Match.

$\frac{3}{4}$ •

•

$\frac{1}{2}$ •

•

$\frac{2}{3}$ •

•

$\frac{1}{3}$ •

•

$\frac{1}{4}$ •

•

Divide the drawings into equal parts.

11.   2 equal parts   **12.**   3 equal parts   **13.**   4 equal parts

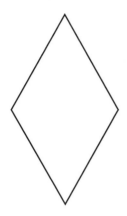 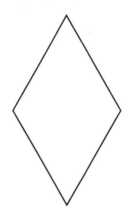 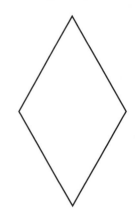

Fill in the blanks.

14.

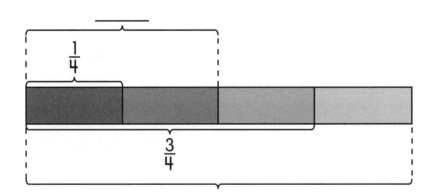

_____

Add or subtract.
Use the model in Exercise 14 to help you.

15. $\frac{1}{4} + \frac{3}{4} =$ _____   **16.** $\frac{1}{4} + \frac{2}{4} =$ _____

17. $1 - \frac{1}{4} =$ _____   **18.** $\frac{3}{4} - \frac{2}{4} =$ _____

Cumulative Review

for Chapters 10 to 12

Concepts and Skills

1. Connect the cards to show the steps for mental math.

| 64 + 8 | 64 − 8 | 84 + 6 | 84 − 6 |

| Add 10 to 64 | Subtract 10 from 64 | Add 10 to 84 | Subtract 10 from 84 |

| Subtract 2 from the result | Subtract 4 from the result | Add 2 to the result | Add 4 to the result |

78 72 90 56

Add mentally.

2. 352 + 4 = _____

3. 817 + 5 = _____

4. 143 + 30 = _____

5. 198 + 800 = _____

Subtract mentally.

6. 916 – 5 = _____

7. 873 – 8 = _____

8. 477 – 60 = _____

9. 858 – 400 = _____

Mark each number with an X on the number line. Then round each number to the nearest ten.

10. 76

11. 81

12. 123

13. 134

Complete.

14. Write the numbers that give 50 when rounded to the nearest ten.

_____

15. What is the least number that rounds to 10? _____

16. What is the greatest number that rounds to 80? _____

Add or subtract.
Round each number to the nearest ten.
Then estimate the sum or difference to check that your answer is reasonable.

17.   874 + 67 = _____

874 is about _____.

67 is about _____.

_____ + _____ = _____.

So, 874 + 67 is about _____.

Is the answer reasonable? Explain.

_____

_____

18.   545 – 79 = _____

545 is about _____.

79 is about _____.

_____ – _____ = _____.

So, 545 – 79 is about _____.

Is the answer reasonable? Explain.

_____

_____

Circle the bills that make the amount shown.

19.

Write the amount in numbers.

20. twenty-five cents $_____ or _____¢

21. thirty-nine dollars $_____

22. twelve dollars and ninety-seven cents $_____

Count the money.
Then write the amount each way.

23.

dollars and cents _____

cents _____

words _____

Name: _____   Date: _____

Circle the amount that is least.

24.　$10.75　　　$7.98　　　$8.07

Circle the greatest amount.

25.　$96.50　　　$96.72　　　$96.09

Shade the model to show the fraction.

26.　$\dfrac{2}{3}$　

27.　$\dfrac{1}{4}$　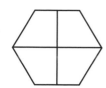

Look at the model.

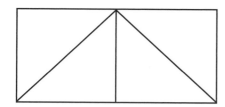

　　Color $\dfrac{1}{4}$ blue.

　　Color $\dfrac{2}{4}$ yellow.

28.　What fraction of the model is colored? _____

29.　What fraction of the model is not colored? _____

Shade each strip.
Then write the fractions in order from greatest to least.

30. $\frac{1}{3}$

$\frac{1}{2}$

$\frac{1}{4}$

————, ————, ————
greatest

Write a fraction for the shaded part.

31.    ————

32.   ————

33.   ————

Use your answers for Exercises 31 to 33. Fill in the blanks.

34. _____ is 1 out of 2 equal parts.

35. _____ is 2 out of 3 equal parts.

36. $\frac{1}{2}$ is greater than _____.

37. $\frac{1}{2}$ is less than _____.

38. _____ is the least fraction.

**Find the missing fraction.
Use models to help you.**

39. Add $\frac{1}{3}$ and $\frac{1}{3}$.

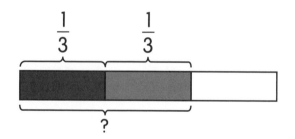

$\frac{1}{3} + \frac{1}{3} =$ _____

40. Subtract $\frac{3}{4}$ from 1.

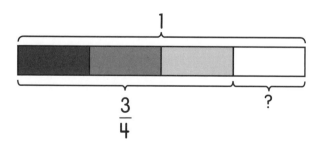

$1 - \frac{3}{4} =$ _____

Solve.
Draw bar models to help you.
Estimate to check your answers.

41. Teri folds 32 pieces of paper.
Her sister folds 19 pieces.
How many pieces do they fold in all?

They fold _____ pieces in all.

42. Edwin has 83¢.
His father gives him 25¢ more.
How much does he have now?

He has $_____ now.

43. Jonas needs to deliver 34 newspapers.
He still has 11 newspapers left to deliver.
How many newspapers has he delivered?

He has delivered _____ newspapers.

44. Adam wants to buy a bat for $23 and a baseball glove for $17.
He has saved $19.
How much more money does he need?

He needs $_____ more.

45. An eraser costs 16¢ and a pencil costs 70¢.
Marian buys two erasers and a pencil.
How much does she spend?

Marian spends $_____.

46. Mrs. Barry has $200 to buy new clothes.
Round the cost of each item to the nearest ten.
Then estimate the total cost.

A pair of pants costs $44.

a. 44 is _____ when rounded to the nearest ten.

A pair of shoes costs $59.

b. 59 is _____ when rounded to the nearest ten.

A pair of socks costs $5.

c. 5 is _____ when rounded to the nearest ten.

A blouse costs $28.

d. 28 is _____ when rounded to the nearest ten.

Total cost is $_____.

Does Mrs. Barry have enough money to pay for all the items?
Explain your answer.

_____

_____

 Customary Measurement of Length

Practice 1   Measuring in Feet

Look at the pictures.
Fill in the blanks with *more* or *less*.

1.

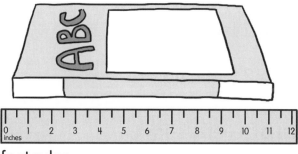

foot ruler

The length of the book

is _____ than 1 foot.

2.

foot rulers

The height of the bag

is _____ than 1 foot.

3.

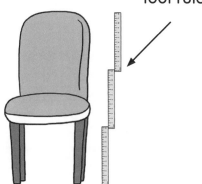

The height of the chair

is _____ than 2 feet.

Fill in the blanks.

4. Foot rulers are placed against two ribbons.

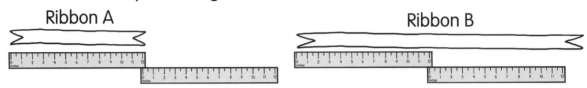

Ribbon A   Ribbon B

a. Which ribbon is about 1 foot long? _____

Fill in the blanks with *more* or *less*.

b. Ribbon A is _____ than 2 feet long.

c. Ribbon B is _____ than 2 feet long.

5. Foot rulers are placed against a bulletin board.

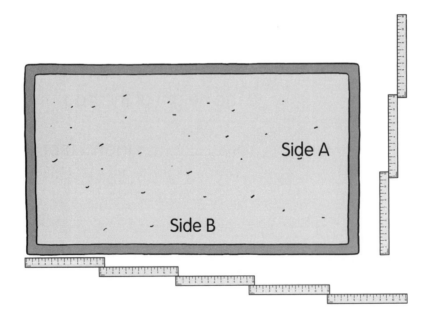

Side A

Side B

a. Which side of the board is about 5 feet long? _____

b. Side A is shorter than _____ feet.

c. Side B is shorter than _____ feet.

Name: _____   Date: _____

Look at the list.
Check (✓) the columns that are true.
You will need a foot ruler to measure these items.

	Item	Less than 1 foot	More than 1 foot	More than 3 feet
6.	Umbrella 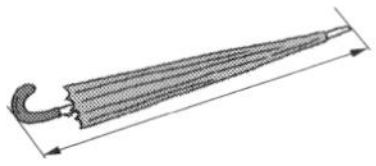			
7.	Blackboard 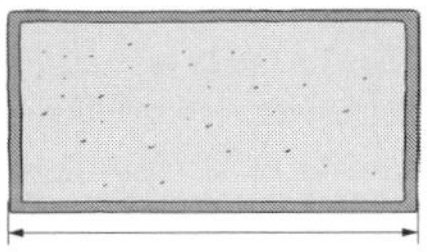			
8.	Shoe 			
9.	Tissue box 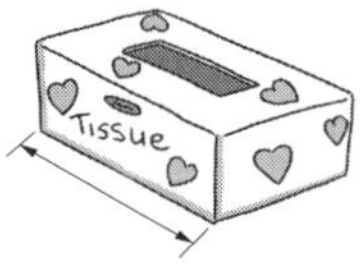			
10.	Bookshelf 			

Look around the classroom to find and name objects that match each length.

11.

Length	Object
Less than 1 foot long	
About 1 foot long	
More than 1 foot long	

Use a string and a foot ruler to measure.
Then fill in the blanks.

12.   Mark on the string with a pencil how long you think 1 foot is.
Then use a ruler to measure this length.
Did you mark more or less than 1 foot on your string?

_____

13.   Next, mark on the string how long you think 2 feet is.
Then use a ruler to measure this length.
Did you mark more or less than 2 feet on your string?

_____

Practice 2   Comparing Lengths in Feet

Fill in the blanks.

1.   Look at the two jump ropes.

 Jump Rope A: 10 ft

 Jump Rope B: 5 ft

a.   Which jump rope is longer? Jump Rope _____

b.   How much longer is it? _____ ft

2.   Look at the trees.

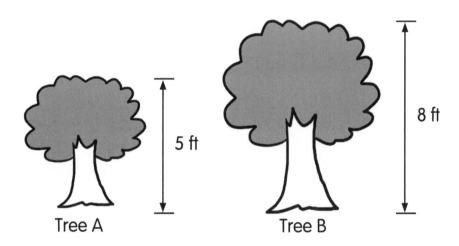

8 ft

5 ft

Tree A   Tree B

a.   Which tree is taller? Tree _____

b.   How much taller is it? _____ ft

Answer the questions.
Look at the sides of the rectangle.

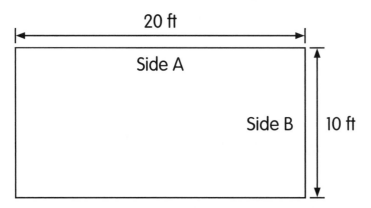

20 ft

Side A

Side B | 10 ft

3. Which is longer, Side A or Side B? Side _____

4. How much longer is it? _____ ft

5. Look at the paths.

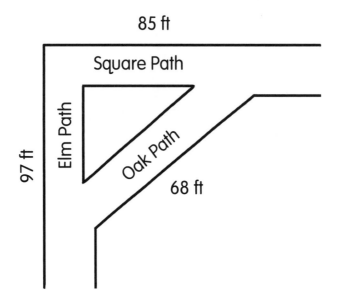

85 ft

Square Path

Elm Path

97 ft

Oak Path

68 ft

a. Which path is the longest? _____

b. How much longer is Elm Path than Square Path? _____ ft

c. Elm Path is _____ feet longer than Oak Path.

Practice 3   Measuring in Inches

1.   Check (✓) the correct way to measure the length of the pencil.

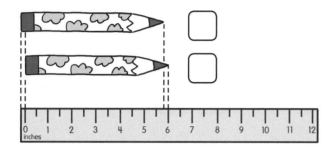

☐

☐

Use an inch ruler to measure each part of a line.
Then answer the questions.

Part of a line A ├───────────────────────────────┤

Part of a line B ├─────────────────────────────────────┤

2.   How long is Part of a line A? _____ in.

3.   How long is Part of a line B? _____ in.

Use a string and an inch ruler to measure each curve.

4.      _____ in.

5.      _____ in.

Fill in the blanks.

6.

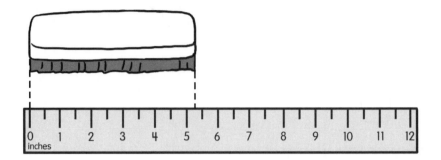

The eraser is about _____ inches long.

7.

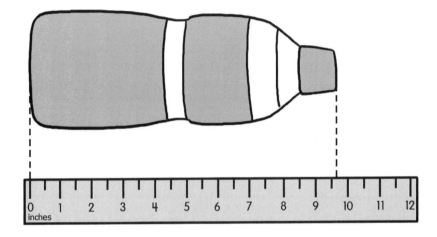

The bottle is about _____ inches long.

8.

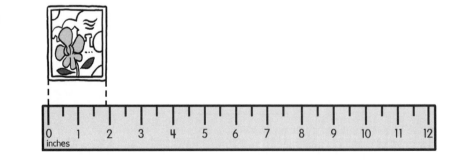

The sticker is about _____ inches long.

Fill in the blanks.

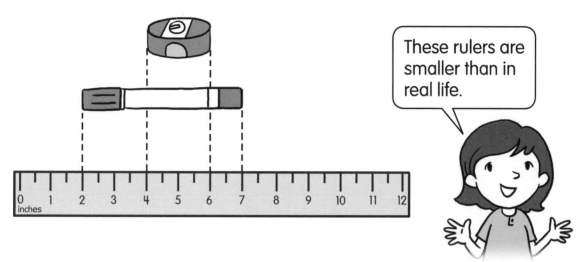

These rulers are smaller than in real life.

9. The marker is _____ inches long.

10. The pencil sharpener is _____ inches long.

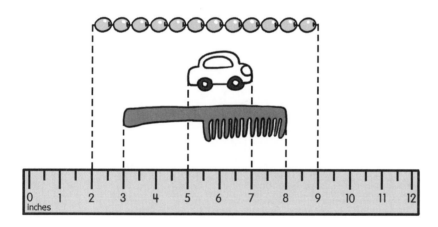

11. The length of the comb is _____ inches.

12. The length of the string of beads is _____ inches.

13. The length of the toy car is _____ inches.

Use your inch ruler to draw.

14. Part of a line A that is 4 inches long.

15. Part of a line B that is 2 inches long.

16. Part of a line C that is 5 inches long.

17. Part of a line D that is 1 inch long.

18. Part of a line E that is 2 inches shorter than Part of a line C.

19. Part of a Line F that is 3 inches longer than Part of a line D.

Practice 4   Comparing Lengths in Inches and Feet

Look at each drawing.
Then fill in the blanks.

1.   Which is longer? Drawing _____

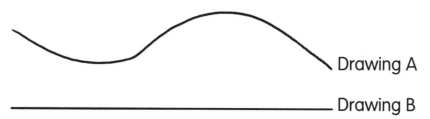

Drawing A

Drawing B

2.   Which is the longest?

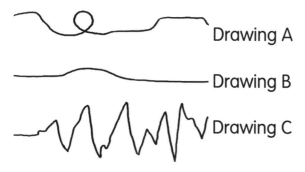

Drawing A

Drawing B

Drawing C

Drawing _____ is the shortest.

Drawing _____ is the longest.
Explain your answers.

_____

_____

_____

Fill in the blanks.

3.

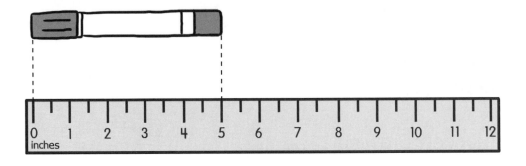

The marker is _____ inches long.

4.

The eraser is _____ inch long.

5.

The key is _____ inches long.

These rulers are smaller than in real life.

Fill in the blanks.

6.

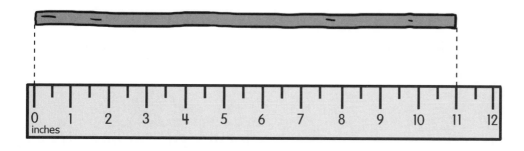

The stick is _____ inches long.

7.

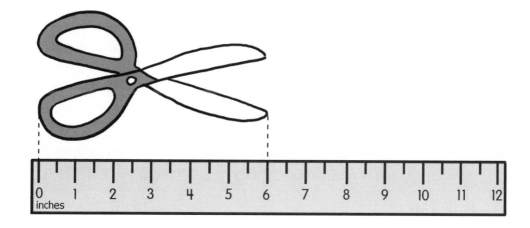

The pair of scissors is _____ inches long.

Use your answers for Exercises 3 to 7.
Fill in the blanks with *longer* or *shorter.*

8. The stick is _____ than the eraser.

9. The key is _____ than the scissors.

10. The eraser is _____ than the marker.

**Use your answers for Exercises 3 to 7.
Fill in the blanks.**

11. The pair of scissors is _____ inches longer
    than the key.

12. The marker is _____ inches shorter than the stick.

13. The longest object is the _____.

14. The shortest object is the _____.

**Measure each object in inches.
Then measure it in feet.**

	Measure (in.)	Measure (ft)
the length of your book		
the width of your hand		
the height of a bookshelf		
the height of a chair		

15. Which objects are easier to measure in inches?

16. Which objects are easier to measure in feet?

17. Why are there more inches than feet when you measure the
    same object?

Practice 5 Real-World Problems: Customary Length

Solve.

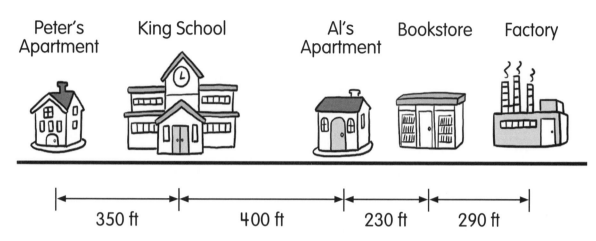

| Peter's Apartment | King School | Al's Apartment | Bookstore | Factory |

350 ft   400 ft   230 ft   290 ft

1. How far does Al walk from his home to
King School?   _____ ft

2. How far is Peter's Apartment from the Bookstore?   _____ ft

3. Who lives nearer to King School, Al or Peter?   _____

4. How much nearer?   _____ ft

5. Al goes to the Bookstore from his apartment, and then
goes to school. How far does he walk?   _____ ft

6. Peter left his apartment to walk to Al's Apartment.
He has walked 400 feet.
How much farther does he have to walk?   _____ ft

Solve.

7. A flagpole is 6 feet tall.
    It stands on a building 26 feet tall.
    How high is the top of the flagpole from the ground?

    The top of the flagpole is _____ feet from the ground.

8. A rope is cut into 3 pieces.
    The rope pieces measure 14 feet, 16 feet, and 20 feet.
    How long was the rope before it was cut?

    The rope was _____ feet long.

9. A flagpole 156 inches tall is driven into the ground.
    38 inches of it is below the ground.
    How much of the flag pole is above the ground?

    _____ inches of the flagpole is above the ground.

Name: _____   Date: _____

Solve.
Show your work.
Use bar models to help you.

Example

The total length of two pieces of wood is 36 feet.
The first piece is 27 feet long.

a. What is the length of the second piece?

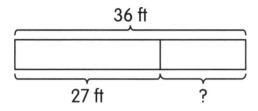

The length of the second piece is ____9____ feet.

b. How much shorter is the second piece than the first piece?

27 − 9 = 18

The second piece is ____18____ feet shorter than the first piece.

10. James is 57 inches tall.
James is 8 inches taller than Ron.
Ron is taller than Brian by 2 inches.
How tall is Brian?

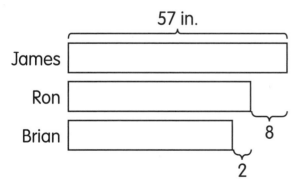

Brian is _____ inches tall.

11. Marcus keeps 3 rolls of cable measuring 67 feet in all.
The first roll is 32 feet.
The second roll is 17 feet.
How long is the third roll?

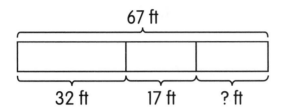

67 ft

32 ft   17 ft   ? ft

The third roll is _____ feet long.

Solve.
Show your work.
Draw bar models to help you.

12. A string is 500 inches long.
Nicole uses 142 inches of it to tie a package.
She gives 75 inches of it to Susan.
How long is the string that Nicole has left?

The string is _____ inches long.

Put On Your Thinking Cap!

Challenging Practice

1. There are three drawings, A, B, and C.
    Drawing A is shown.

    ├──────────────────────────────┤ Drawing A

    Drawing B is 12 inches longer than Drawing A.
    Drawing C is 4 inches shorter than Drawing B.
    How long is Drawing C?

2. Tom and Lionel climb a tree.
    They have to climb a ladder first, then up to the branches.
    The ladder is 6 feet long.
    Tom climbs 4 feet from the ladder to a branch.
    Lionel climbs 2 feet from the ladder to another branch.
    What is the total distance that Tom and Lionel have climbed?

Put On Your Thinking Cap!

Problem Solving

Solve.

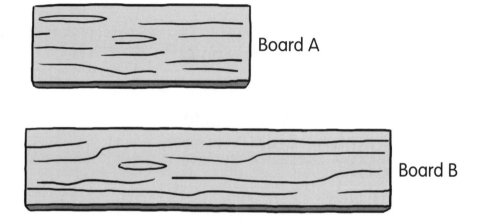

Board A

Board B

There are 2 boards, A and B.

The total length of both boards is 28 feet.

Board B is at least 5 feet longer than Board A, but the difference is not more than 12 feet.

What are the possible lengths of the two boards?

Chapter Review/Test
Vocabulary

Fill in the blanks with words from the box.

foot/feet
_____
inch/inches
_____
tallest
_____
shorter

1. Measure short lengths in _____

   and longer lengths in _____.

2.

   A   B   C

   Cookie jar C is the _____.

3. 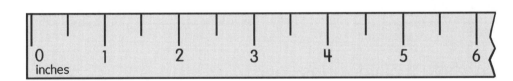 Simone's

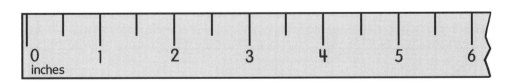 Annie's

   Annie's string of beads is 2 inches _____ than Simone's.

Concepts and Skills

Check (✔) the correct answers.

4. What is the length of your math textbook?

Length	Check
About 1 foot	
Less than 1 foot	
More than 1 foot	

5. What is the height of your desk?

Height	Check
About 2 feet	
Less than 2 feet	
More than 3 feet	
Less than 3 feet	

6. What is the height of your classroom?

Height	Check
About 20 feet	
Less than 20 feet	
More than 10 feet	
Less than 10 feet	

Name: _____ **Date:** _____

Look at the objects measured.
Then fill in the blanks.

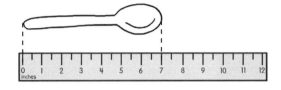

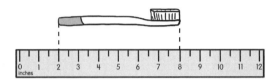

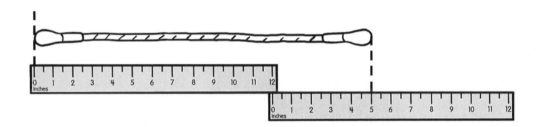

7. spoon: _____ in.

8. toothbrush: _____ in.

9. rope: _____ ft _____ in.

10. The rope is _____ foot longer than the spoon.

11. The rope is longer than _____ foot.

12.

The photo is about _____ inches long.

13. Use a ruler to draw a part of a line 7 inches long.

Problem Solving

Solve.
Show your work.
Draw bar models to help you.

14. Ms. Cooper used 86 feet of yellow yarn and 123 feet of blue yarn to make a sweater.

    a. What is the total length of yarn that Ms. Cooper used to make a sweater?

        The total length of yarn is _____ feet.

    b. How much more blue yarn than yellow yarn did Ms. Cooper use?

        Ms. Cooper used _____ feet more blue yarn than yellow yarn.

15. A bookshelf is 50 inches tall.
It is 15 inches shorter than a step ladder.
How tall is the ladder?

    The step ladder is _____ inches tall.

Time

Practice 1   The Minute Hand

1.   Fill in the boxes with the number of minutes.

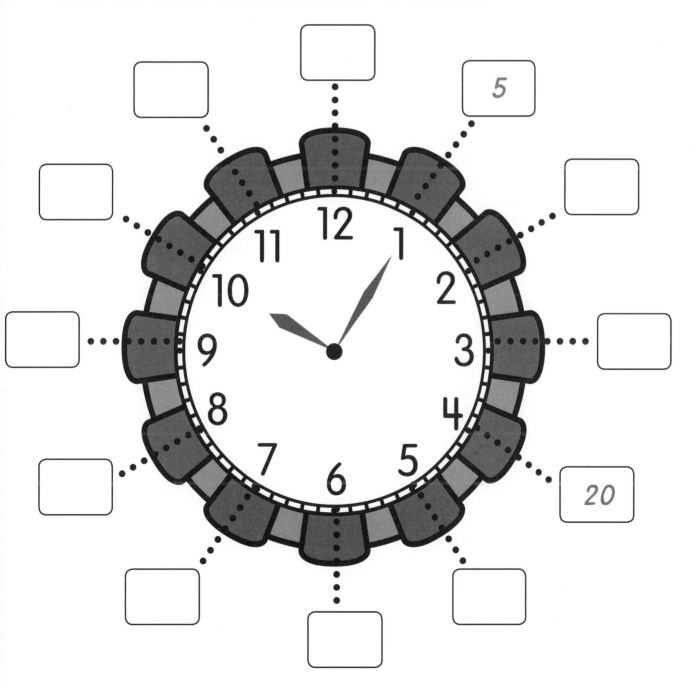

Fill in the blanks.

Example

The minute hand points to ____30____ minutes.

The minute hand is longer than the hour hand.

2.

The minute hand points to _____ minutes.

3.

The minute hand points to _____ minutes.

4.

The minute hand points to _____ minutes.

Write the time.

5.

_____   _____ minutes after 3 o'clock.

6.

_____   _____ minutes after 7 o'clock.

7.

_____   _____ minutes after 10 o'clock.

Draw the minute hand to show the time.

8.   15 minutes after 4 o'clock

9.   40 minutes after 6 o'clock

10.   50 minutes after 1 o'clock

11.   35 minutes after 10 o'clock

Practice 2   Reading and Writing Time

Write the time in words.

┌─ **Example** ─────────────────┐

ten fifty or 50 minutes after 10
└───────────────────────────────┘

1.

_____

2.

_____

3.

_____

4.

_____

5.

_____

Write the time.

The time is __7:40__.

6.

The time is _____.

7.

The time is _____.

8.

The time is _____.

9.

The time is _____.

10.

The time is _____.

Draw the minute hand to show the time.

Example

The time is 3:55.

11.

The time is 6:30.

12.

The time is 10:15.

13.

The time is 8:00.

14.

The time is 12:40.

15.

The time is 9:05.

Draw the hour hand to show the time.

Example

The time is 10:00.

16.

The time is 11:30.

17.

The time is 7:15.

18.

The time is 4:20.

19.

The time is 2:50.

20.

The time is 3:40.

Draw the hands to show the time.

Example

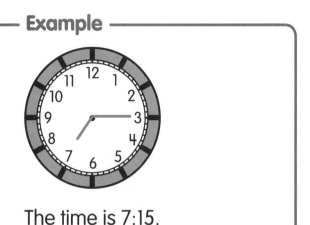

The time is 7:15.

21.

The time is 4:30.

22.

The time is 1:20.

23.

The time is 9:25.

24.

The time is 7:00.

25.

The time is 9:50.

Draw the hands to show the time.
Then write the time in words.

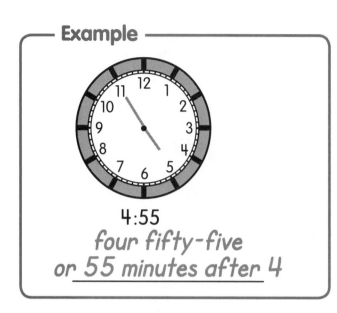

4:55
four fifty-five
or 55 minutes after 4

26.

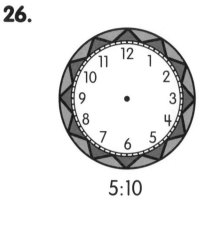

5:10

_____

27.

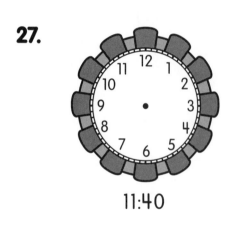

11:40

_____

28.

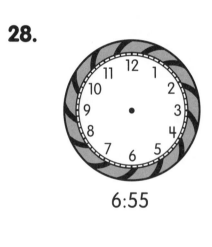

6:55

_____

29.

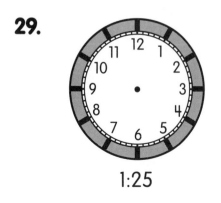

1:25

_____

30.

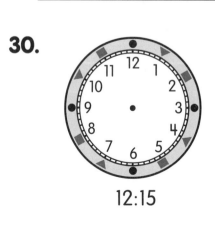

12:15

_____

Practice 3   Using A.M. and P.M.

Write A.M. or P.M.

> **Example**
>
>
>
> Sam wakes up at 6:30 __A.M.__

1.

His grandparents begin their

daily exercise at 6:50 _____

2.

Sometimes, Sam rides his bike in

the afternoon at 2:50 _____

Write *A.M.* **or** *P.M.*

3. The sun sets at

about 7:25 _____

4.

At 6:30 _____, Sam eats

his dinner with his friend.

5.

His father likes to go jogging at night.

He usually jogs at 8:30 _____

6. Denise and her mother finished grocery shopping at 10:30 _____

7. The family had lunch at 12:30 _____

8. They reached home at 11:00 _____

Write A.M. or P.M.

9. Denise woke up at 7:30 _____

10. Denise and her mother left for the grocery store at 9:30 _____

11. Denise helped her mother put away the groceries. Then they started preparing lunch at 11:30 _____

12. List the times of events in Practice 6–11. Arrange them in order from the beginning of the day.

_____

Beginning

Name: _____   Date: _____

Practice 4   Elapsed Time

Fill in the blanks with the time.

Check your answer by drawing the hands on the clock.

Example

   is 1 hour after

_5:00_   _4:00_

1.

   is 1 hour before

11:00   _____

2.

   is 1 hour after

8:00   _____

Write *before* or *after*.

 is 1 hour ___*before*___

3.

 is 1 hour _____

4.

 is 1 hour _____

5.

 is 1 hour _____

Name: _____   **Date:** _____

Fill in the blanks with the time.

Check your answer by drawing the hands on the clock.

   is 30 minutes before

_1:30_   _2:00_

6.

   is 30 minutes after

_____   8:00

7.

   is 30 minutes before

_____   10:00

Write *before* or *after*.

 is 30 minutes __*after*__

8.

 is 30 minutes _____

9.

 is 30 minutes _____

10.

 is 30 minutes _____

Name: _____

Date: _____

Draw the hands on the clock.
Then write the time.

11.

is 30 minutes after

_____

_____

12.

is 1 hour after

_____

_____

13.

is 30 minutes before

_____

_____

Write *before* or *after*.

Then draw the hands on the clock.

14.

7:00

is 1 hour _____

6:00

15.

6:30

is 1 hour _____

7:30

16.

6:00

is 30 minutes _____

6:30

Fill in the blanks with the number of minutes or hours.

17. Captain James left the dock at 8.00 A.M. and arrived on shore at 8:30 A.M.

Start

End

How long was the trip? _____

18. Peter played basketball from 6.00 P.M. to 7.00 P.M.

Start

End

How long did he play? _____

Math Journal

Find the mistakes.
Circle the mistakes.
Then correct them.

1.

Albert wrote: The time is 4:25.

_____

2. Keisha drew the hands on the clock
to show 7:55.
This is how she did it.

Put On Your Thinking Cap!

Challenging Practice

Look at the picture.
Where can the hour hand be?
Draw it on the clock face.
Explain.

Put On Your Thinking Cap!

Problem Solving

What time did Kyle finish his homework?
Use the clues below to find out.

> Kyle spent 1 hour writing his story.
> He took another 30 minutes to color the pictures.
> Kyle started his homework at 6.00 P.M.

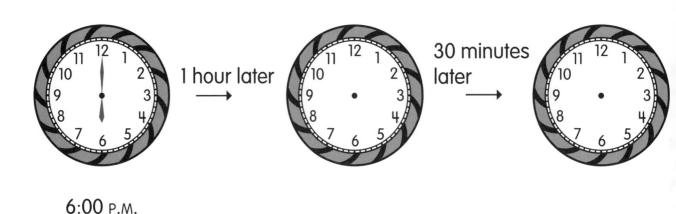

__6:00__ P.M.   1 hour later →   30 minutes later →

_____   _____

Chapter Review/Test

Vocabulary

Fill in the blanks with words from the box.

| minutes | hours | A.M. | P.M. |

1. 60 _____ is equal to 1 hour.

2. Use _____ to talk about time just after midnight to just
before noon.

3. Use _____ to talk about time just after noon to just
before midnight.

4. Use a clock to tell time in _____ and minutes.

Concepts and Skills

Write the time in numbers and in words.

5.

_____

_____

6.

_____

_____

Draw the hands on the clock to show the time.

7.

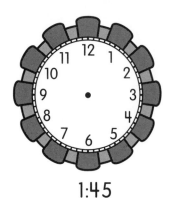

1:45

8.

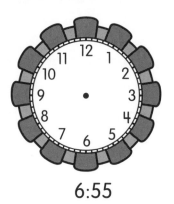

6:55

Write A.M. or P.M.

9. Katy goes to school at 7:15 _____

10. She goes home after school at 3:00 _____

Find the time.

11. 30 minutes before 6:00 P.M. is _____

12. 30 minutes after noon is _____

13. 1 hour before 3:30 A.M. is _____

14. 1 hour after midnight is _____

Problem Solving

Solve.

15. Annie spent 30 minutes on her math homework.
She started at 6:30 P.M.
What time did she finish? _____

16. Pedro has swimming lesson from 5:00 P.M.
to 6:00 P.M. How long is his swimming lesson? _____

Name: _____   Date: _____

Cumulative Review

for Chapters 13 and 14

Concepts and Skills

Fill in the blanks.

foot ruler

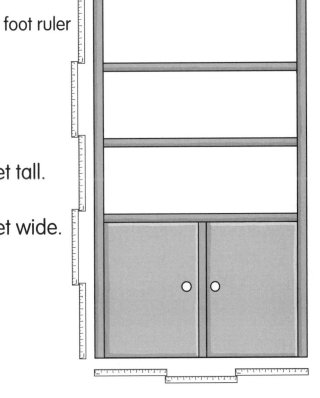

1.   The bookshelf is _____ feet tall.

2.   The bookshelf is _____ feet wide.

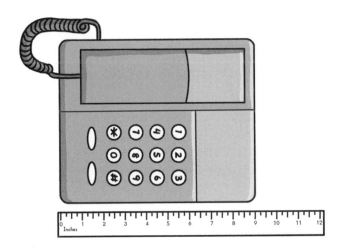

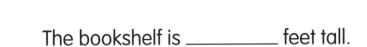

3.   The telephone is _____ inches long.

Fill in the blanks with *feet* or *inches*.

4. A car is about 8 _____ long.

5. The grip on a bicycle handle bar is about 6 _____ long.

Look at each drawing.
Then fill in the blanks.

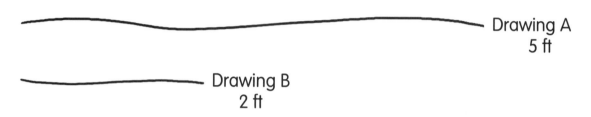

Drawing A
5 ft

Drawing B
2 ft

6. Which drawing is shorter? _____

7. How much shorter? _____ feet

Fill in the blanks.

8. The tree is about _____ feet shorter than the house.

9. The tree is about _____ feet tall.

Name: _____   Date: _____

Side A
12 in.

←—Side B—→
7 in.

10. Side A is _____ inches longer than Side B.

11. The total length of the two sides is _____.

Use the picture to answer each question.

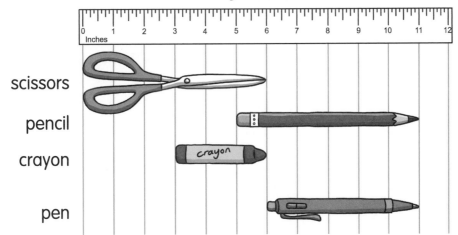

scissors

pencil

crayon

pen

12. What is the length of the pen? _____

13. Which is longer, the scissors or the pen? _____

14. The shortest item is the _____.

15. Which two items have the same length? _____

16. The total length of 2 pens and 3 crayons is _____ inches.

17. The length of _____ crayons is more than the length of 2 pens.

Draw the hands to show the time.
Then fill in the blanks.

18.

The time is 4:15.

It is 15 minutes after _____ o'clock.

19.

The time is 9:55.

It is _____ minutes after 9 o'clock.

20.

The time is 6:45.

It is _____ minutes after 6 o'clock.

21.

The time is 11:15.

It is 15 minutes after _____ o'clock.

Match.
Then write the time in words under each digital clock.

22.

6:45

_____

5:30

23.

24.

_____

2:20

_____

3:10

25.

26.

_____

1:15

_____

4:05

27.

_____

Fill in the blanks with *A.M.* or *P.M.*

28. On Saturdays, Marjorie usually wakes up at 8:00 _____

29. She has lunch at her grandparents' house at 12:30 _____

30. She helps her mother do house chores at 9:30 _____

31. She plays board games with her grandpa at 3:00 _____

32. She goes home at 5:00 _____

Now list the times in Exercises 28 to 32 in order from the beginning of the day.

33. _____   _____   _____
Beginning

_____   _____

Fill in the blanks with the time.
Check your answer by drawing the hands on the clock.

34.

   is 1 hour after   

1:00   _____

35.

is 1 hour before

_____

10:30

36.

is 30 minutes after

_____

11:00

37.

is 30 minutes before

2:00

_____

Fill in the blanks with *before* or *after*.

38.

   is 1 hour _____

39.

   is 1 hour _____

40.

   is 30 minutes _____

41.

   is 30 minutes _____

Problem Solving

Solve.
Draw bar models to help you.

42.   Ben uses a piece of rope to form a triangle.

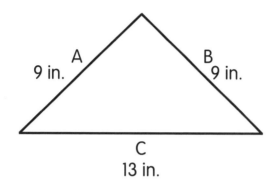

9 in. A

B 9 in.

C
13 in.

   a.   What is the length of the rope?
   b.   How much longer is the sum of the two shorter sides than the longest side of the triangle?

   a.   The rope is _____ inches long.

   b.   The sum of the two shorter sides is _____ inches longer than the longest side.

43.   Rope A is 56 feet long.
   Rope B is 47 feet longer than Rope A.
   Rope C is 71 feet shorter than Rope B.

   a.   How long is Rope B?
   b.   How long is Rope C?

   a.   Rope B is _____ feet long.

   b.   Rope C is _____ feet long.

44. Jason is 71 inches tall.
Rodney is 12 inches shorter than Jason.
Marco is 18 inches taller than Rodney.

   a. How tall is Rodney?

   b. How tall is Marco?

   a. Rodney is _____ inches tall.

   b. Marco is _____ inches tall.

45.

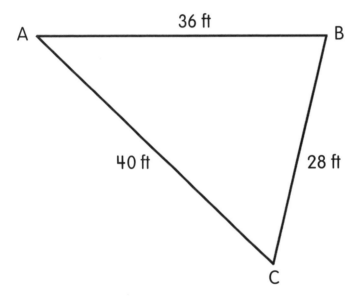

   a. Adam walks from Point A to Point C through Point B.

      How far does he walk? _____

   b. Susan walks from Point B to Point C through Point A.

      How far does she walk? _____

   c. Who walks farther? _____

      How much farther? _____

Name: _____   Date: _____

Multiplication Tables of 3 and 4

Practice 1   Multiplying 3: Skip-Counting

Match the shapes that have the same value.

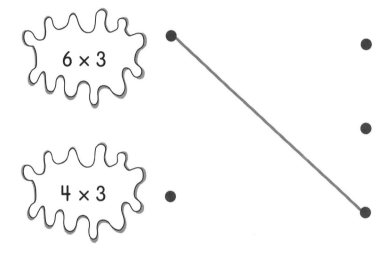

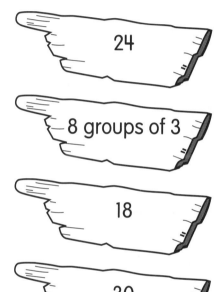

6 × 3

24

8 groups of 3

1.
4 × 3

18

2.
5 × 3

30

12

3.
10 × 3

15

4.
8 × 3

10 groups of 3

4 groups of 3

Count by 3s.
Then fill in the blanks.

Example

3, 6, 9, 12, __*15*__, 18

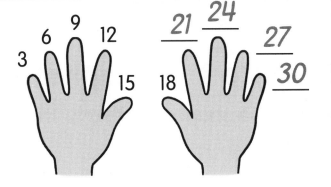

5. 9, 12, 15, _____, _____, _____, _____

6. 12, _____, 18, 21, _____, _____, 30

Fill in the blanks.

7. $4 \times 3 =$ _____

8. $2 \times 3 =$ _____

9. $6 \times 3 =$ _____

10. $8 \times 3 =$ _____

11. $9 \times 3 =$ _____

12. $7 \times 3 =$ _____

13. $3 \times 3 =$ _____

14. $10 \times 3 =$ _____

Solve.

15. Andrea has 5 flower vases.
Each vase has 3 roses.
How many roses are there in all?

$5 \times 3 =$ _____

There are _____ roses in all.

Practice 2   Multiplying 3: Using Dot Paper

Use dot paper to solve.

Example

Sally buys 4 lanterns.
Each lantern costs $3.
How much does Sally pay for the lanterns?

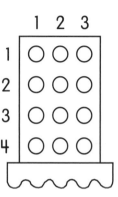

4 × $3 = $_____*12*_____

Sally pays $_____*12*_____ for the lanterns.

---

1.   Nicole buys 6 soup bowls.
Each soup bowl costs $3.
How much does she pay for all the soup bowls?

_____ × $3 = $_____

She pays $_____ for all the soup bowls.

Use dot paper to solve.

2. There are 7 tricycles.
Each tricycle has 3 wheels.
How many wheels are there in all?

_____ × _____ = _____

There are _____ wheels in all.

3. There are 8 groups of children in the class.
There are 3 children in each group.
How many children are there in the class?

_____ × _____ = _____

There are _____ children in the class.

Use dot paper to help you fill in the blanks.

Example

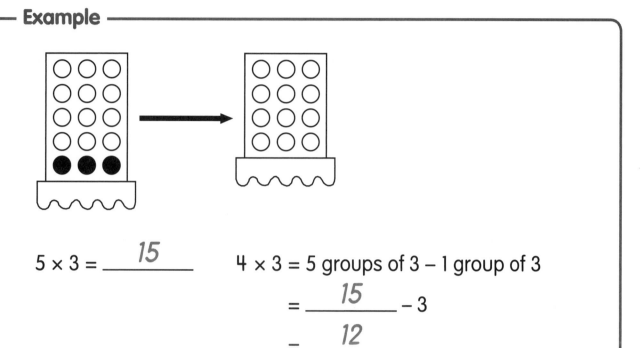

$5 \times 3 =$ ___15___

$4 \times 3 = 5$ groups of $3 - 1$ group of 3

$= $ ___15___ $- 3$

$= $ ___12___

4.

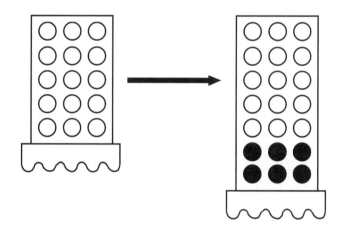

$5 \times 3 =$ _____

$7 \times 3 = 5$ groups of $3 +$ _____ groups of 3

$= $ _____ $+$ _____

$= $ _____

Use dot paper to help you fill in the blanks.

5.

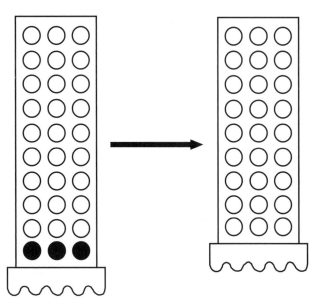

10 × 3 = _____   9 × 3 = 10 groups of 3 – _____ group of 3

= _____ – _____

= _____

6.

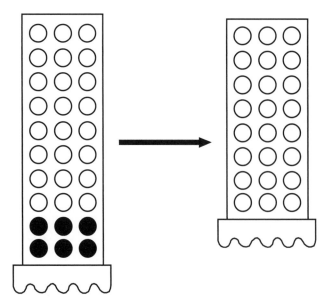

10 × 3 = _____   8 × 3 = 10 groups of 3 – _____ groups of 3

= _____ – _____

= _____

Name: _____ Date: _____

Use dot paper to help you fill in the blanks.

Example

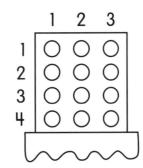
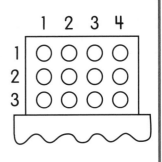

_____4_____ × 3 = 12

3 × _____4_____ = 12

---

7. _____ × 3 = 18

3 × _____ = 18

8. _____ × 3 = 21

3 × _____ = 21

9. 8 × 3 = _____

3 × 8 = _____

10. _____ × 3 = 27

3 × _____ = 27

Math Journal

These items are sold in a supermarket.
Use the items to write a multiplication story.

$3

$4

Example

I want to buy 4 boxes of cereal.

I will have to give the cashier $16.

Story

Practice 3 Multiplying 4: Skip-Counting

Match.

8 × 4

□————————————————□ 4 groups of 4

1.

7 × 4

●   ● 2 groups of 4

2.

2 × 4

●   ● 7 groups of 4

3.

4 × 4

●————————————————● 8 groups of 4

Count by 4s.
Then fill in the blanks.

Example

4, 8, 12, 16, _____20_____

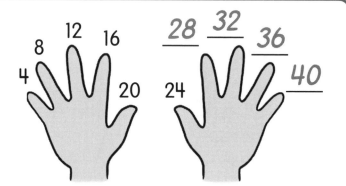

4. 12, 16, 20, _____, _____, _____, _____

5. 16, _____, 24, 28, _____, _____, 40

Fill in the blanks.

6. $3 \times 4 =$ _____

7. $6 \times 4 =$ _____

8. $2 \times 4 =$ _____

9. $8 \times 4 =$ _____

10. $9 \times 4 =$ _____

11. $4 \times 4 =$ _____

12. $10 \times 4 =$ _____

13. $7 \times 4 =$ _____

Solve.

14. There are 5 pencil cases.
4 erasers are in each pencil case.
How many erasers are there in all?

$5 \times 4 =$ _____

There are _____ erasers in all.

Practice 4 Multiplying 4: Using Dot Paper

Solve.

Example

There are 3 boxes of crayons.
There are 4 crayons in each box.
How many crayons are there in all?

   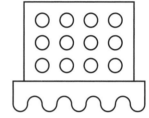

$3 \times 4 =$ ___*12*___

There are ___*12*___ crayons in all.

---

1. There are 6 toy cars in a toy box.
Each car has 4 wheels.
How many wheels are there in all?

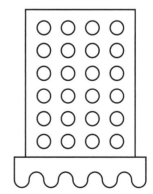

_____ × 4 = _____

There are _____ wheels in all.

Use dot paper to solve.

2. Mrs. Jones buys 5 T-shirts.
Each T-shirt costs $4.
How much does Mrs. Jones spend in all?

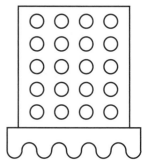

_____ × $4 = $_____

Mrs. Jones spends $_____ in all.

3. There are 8 bags.
Each bag has 4 muffins.
How many muffins are there in all?

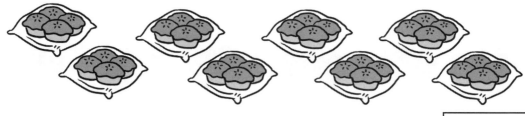

_____ × _____ = _____

There are _____ muffins in all.

Use dot paper to help you fill in the blanks.

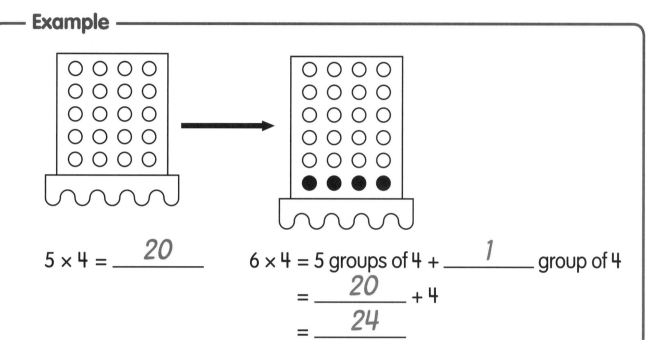

Example

$5 \times 4 =$ _____*20*_____

$6 \times 4 = 5$ groups of $4 +$ _____*1*_____ group of 4

$\quad = $ _____*20*_____ $+ 4$

$\quad = $ _____*24*_____

4.

$10 \times 4 =$ _____

$8 \times 4 = 10$ groups of $4 -$ _____ groups of 4

$\quad = $ _____ $- 8$

$\quad = $ _____

5. $7 \times 4 =$ _____ $+ 8$

$\quad = $ _____

6. $9 \times 4 =$ _____ $- 4$

$\quad = $ _____

Use dot paper to help you fill in the blanks.

Example

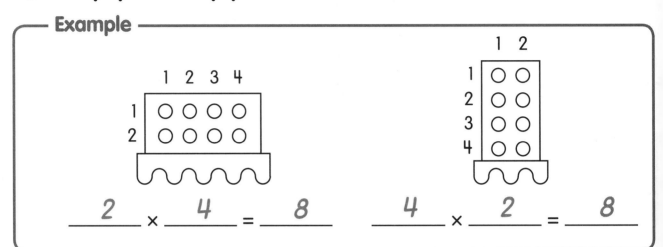

$$\underline{\quad 2 \quad} \times \underline{\quad 4 \quad} = \underline{\quad 8 \quad} \qquad \underline{\quad 4 \quad} \times \underline{\quad 2 \quad} = \underline{\quad 8 \quad}$$

7.

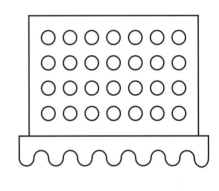

$$\underline{\qquad} \times \underline{\qquad} = \underline{\qquad} \qquad \underline{\qquad} \times \underline{\qquad} = \underline{\qquad}$$

8.

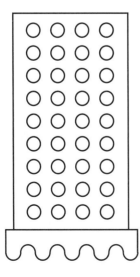 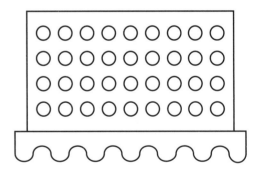

$$\underline{\qquad} \times \underline{\qquad} = \underline{\qquad} \qquad \underline{\qquad} \times \underline{\qquad} = \underline{\qquad}$$

Practice 5   Divide Using Related Multiplication Facts

Complete the multiplication sentences.
Then complete the division sentences.

Example

$24 \div 4 =$ ___6___

$24 \div 3 =$ ___8___

$6 \times 4 = 24$
$8 \times 3 = 24$

---

1. $4 \times$ _____ $= 8$

_____ $\times 4 = 8$

$8 \div 2 =$ _____

$8 \div 4 =$ _____

2. $4 \times$ _____ $= 12$

_____ $\times 4 = 12$

$12 \div 3 =$ _____

$12 \div 4 =$ _____

3. $5 \times$ _____ $= 15$

_____ $\times 5 = 15$

$15 \div 3 =$ _____

$15 \div 5 =$ _____

4. $5 \times$ _____ $= 20$

_____ $\times 5 = 20$

$20 \div 4 =$ _____

$20 \div 5 =$ _____

Use related multiplication facts to solve.

Example

The teacher divides 21 books equally among 3 children.
How many books does each child get?

$$\underline{\quad 21 \quad} \div \underline{\quad 3 \quad} = \underline{\quad 7 \quad}$$

Each child gets __7__ books.

---

5. Mr. Holtz gives $24 to 4 workers.
The workers share the money equally among themselves.
How much money does each worker get?

$$\$\underline{\qquad} \div \underline{\qquad} = \$\underline{\qquad}$$

Each worker gets $_____.

6. Rita has 27 stuffed toys.
She puts them on 3 shelves.
She puts the same number on each shelf.
How many stuffed toys are on each shelf?

$$\underline{\qquad} \div \underline{\qquad} = \underline{\qquad}$$

There are _____ stuffed toys on each shelf.

Use related multiplication facts to solve.

7. Phil puts 36 pencils equally into 4 boxes.
How many pencils are in each box?

_____ ÷ _____ = _____

There are _____ pencils in each box.

8. Angie uses 9 craft sticks to make 3 triangles of the same size.
How many craft sticks are needed to make one triangle?

_____ ÷ _____ = _____

_____ craft sticks are needed to make one triangle.

9. Sammy fixes 8 tires on his cars.
He fixes 4 tires on each car.
How many cars are there?

_____ ÷ _____ = _____

There are _____ cars.

10. Mr. Yuma has 18 pieces of bread.
He puts 3 pieces in each basket.
How many baskets does he use?

_____ ÷ _____ = _____

He uses _____ baskets.

11. A photo album contains 20 photos.
Each filled page of the album has 4 photos.
How many pages are filled?

_____ ÷ _____ = _____

_____ pages are filled.

12. Keisha has 9 fish.
She puts 3 fish in each fish tank.
How many fish tanks does she need?

_____ ÷ _____ = _____

She needs _____ fish tanks.

Put On Your Thinking Cap!

Challenging Practice

1. Steve starts reading a book at page 7.
He reads the book for 4 days.
He reads 3 pages each day.
Which page will Steve stop at on the 4th day?

(Hint: Use a diagram to help you solve.)

2. The music teacher is selecting children to sit in the
front row at a concert.
100 children are given numbers 1 to 100.
The teacher first picks the child with the number 3.
He then skip-counts by tens to pick the other children.
What are the numbers of the other children who are picked?

The numbers are _____.

Put On Your Thinking Cap!

Problem Solving

Solve the riddle.

I am a two-digit number.
I am more than 20 but less than 30.
I can be found in both the multiplication tables
of 3 and 4.
What number am I?

Chapter Review/Test

Vocabulary
Fill in the blanks with words from the box.

1.

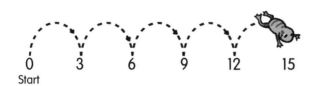

0   3   6   9   12   15
Start

_____ is fun!

skip-counting
dot paper
related multiplication facts

2. $6 \times 3 = 18$ $3 \times 6 = 18$ are examples of

_____.

Concepts and Skills

Skip count to find the missing numbers.

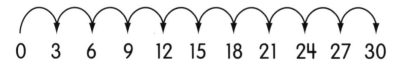

0   3   6   9   12   15   18   21   24   27   30

3. $9 \times 3 =$ _____

4. _____ $\times 3 = 24$

0   4   8   12   16   20   24   28   32   36   40

5. _____ $\times 4 = 16$

6. _____ $\times 4 = 36$

Find the missing numbers.

7.   8 groups of 3 = _____ × 3

   = _____

8.   7 groups of 4 = _____ × 4

   = _____

Use dot paper to find the missing numbers.

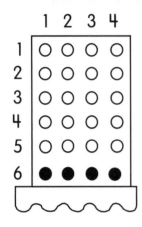

9.   6 × 4 = 5 groups of 4 + _____ group of 4

   = _____ + 4

   = _____

Problem Solving

Use skip-counting or dot paper to solve.

10.   Caleb ties sets of 3 medals with a piece of ribbon.
   He ties 10 sets of medals.
   How many medals does Caleb have in all?

Use related multiplication facts to solve.

11.   Gail has 32 star-shaped key chains.
   She puts 4 key chains equally into some boxes.
   How many boxes are there?

CHAPTER 16 Using Bar Models: Multiplication and Division

Practice 1   Real-World Problems: Multiplication

Solve.
Use bar models to help you.

Example

Aaron has 3 baskets of oranges.
There are 5 oranges in each basket.
How many oranges does Aaron have?

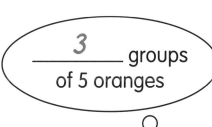

_____3_____ groups
of 5 oranges

5

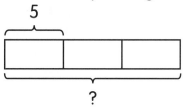

?

_____3_____ × 5 = _____15_____

Aaron has _____15_____ oranges.

---

1.   Susan has 4 bunches of roses.
There are 8 roses in each bunch.
How many roses does Susan have?

_____ groups
of 8 roses

8

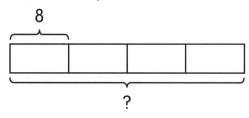

?

_____ × 8 = _____

Susan has _____ roses.

Solve.
Draw bar models to help you.

2. Willie reads 10 pages of his book each day.
How many pages does he read in 3 days?

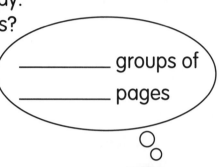

_____ × _____ = _____

Willie reads _____ pages in 3 days.

3. There are 7 boxes.
There are 5 baseballs in each box.
How many baseballs are there in all?

_____ × _____ = _____

There are _____ baseballs in all.

Name: _____ **Date:** _____

Solve.
Draw bar models to help you.

4. There are 3 tricycles in a shop.
Each tricycle has 3 wheels.
How many wheels do the tricycles have in all?

The tricycles have _____ wheels in all.

5. Carlos buys 5 boxes of markers.
There are 10 markers in each box.
How many markers does Carlos buy?

Carlos buys _____ markers.

Solve.
Draw bar models to help you.

6.   There are 9 boxes of rocks.
         There are 3 rocks in each box.
         How many rocks are there in all?

         There are _____ rocks in all.

7.   Samuel makes 6 shapes using craft sticks.
         He uses 5 craft sticks for each shape.
         How many craft sticks does Samuel use in all?

         Samuel uses _____ craft sticks in all.

Solve.
Draw bar models to help you.

8. Farah has 8 vases.
    She puts 5 flowers in each vase.
    How many flowers does Farah have in all?

    Farah has _____ flowers in all.

9. Benny has 7 fish tanks.
    There are 4 goldfish in each tank.
    How many goldfish does Benny have?

    Benny has _____ goldfish.

 **Math Journal**

Fill in the blanks, circles, and ovals.

To show 3 groups of 6 strawberries,

Step 1   I draw _____ strips of equal lengths in a row to represent 3 groups.

Step 2   I write the number _____ in the oval above one strip

and a _____ in the oval below the strips.

Step 3   I write the number sentence.

_____ $\bigcirc$ _____ = ?

Step 4   I _____ to find the answer.

_____ $\bigcirc$ _____ = _____

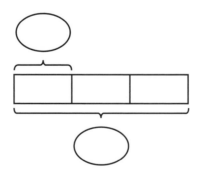

Practice 2   Real-World Problems: Division

Circle the correct bar model.

Example

Divide 15 children into 5 groups.
How many children are in each group?

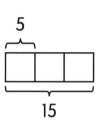   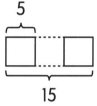   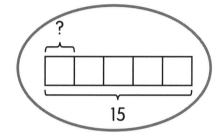

1.   Place 20 strawberries equally on 4 plates.
     How many strawberries are on each plate?

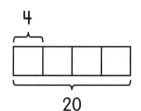   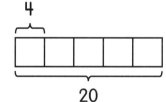   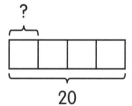

2.   There are 21 buttons to sew on some shirts.
     Each shirt needs 3 buttons.
     How many shirts are there?

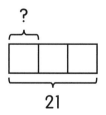   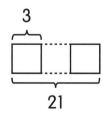   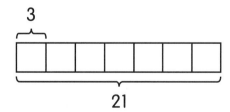

Solve.
Use the bar model to help you.

Example

A baker has 12 rolls.
He divides the rolls equally among 4 children.
How many rolls does each child get?

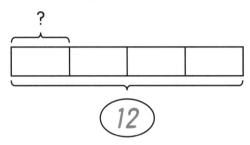

$\underline{\quad 12 \quad} \div \underline{\quad 4 \quad} = \underline{\quad 3 \quad}$

Each child gets $\underline{\quad 3 \quad}$ rolls.

---

3.   Zach has 36 plants and 4 pots.
He puts an equal number of plants in each pot.
How many plants are in each pot?

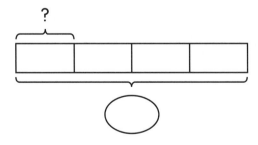

$\underline{\qquad} \div \underline{\qquad} = \underline{\qquad}$

There are $\underline{\qquad}$ plants in each pot.

Solve.
Use the bar model to help you.

— Example —

Ben has 35 leather strips.
He uses 5 strips for each necklace he makes.
How many necklaces does he make?

? necklaces

| 5 | - - - - - - - - - - - - - - - - - | 5 |

35 leather strips

$$\underline{\quad 35 \quad} \div \underline{\quad 5 \quad} = \underline{\quad 7 \quad}$$

Ben makes ____7____ necklaces.

4. Lily sews 24 dresses for her dolls.
Each doll gets 3 dresses.
How many dolls does Lily have?

? dolls

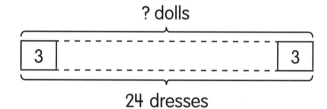

| 3 | - - - - - - - - - - - - - - - - - | 3 |

24 dresses

$$\underline{\qquad} \div \underline{\qquad} = \underline{\qquad}$$

Lily has _____ dolls.

Solve.
Draw bar models to help you.

5.   Gina has 40 stamps.
     She pastes them equally on 4 pages in her album.
     How many stamps are on each page?

     There are _____ stamps on each page.

6.   Ryan has read 28 pages of a book.
     He reads 4 pages each day.
     How many days has Ryan been reading the book?

     Ryan has been reading for _____ days.

Practice 3   Real-World Problems: Measurement and Money

Tell whether you need to multiply or divide.
Then solve.
Use bar models to help you.

Example

Jen walks along an 8-meter path.
She walks along the path 3 times each day.
How far does she walk each day?

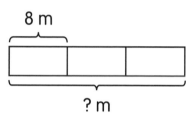

8 m

? m

$8 \times 3 =$ ___24___

Jen walks ___24___ meters each day.

Multiply to find the answer.

---

1.   Raul cuts 6 strips of paper.
Each strip is 5 centimeters long.
He tapes them together to make a long strip.
How long is the strip he makes?

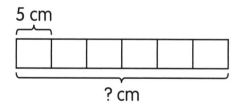

5 cm

? cm

$5 \times 6 =$ _____

The strip is _____ centimeters long.

Tell whether you need to multiply or divide.
Then solve.
Use bar models to help you.

2. Helen has a ribbon that is 21 inches long.
She cuts it into 3 equal pieces.
How long is each piece?

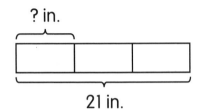

? in.

21 in.

$21 \div 3 =$ _____

Each piece is _____ inches long.

3. Jessica has a string that is 30 feet long.
She cuts it into equal pieces.
Each piece is 5 feet long.
How many pieces does she cut the string into?

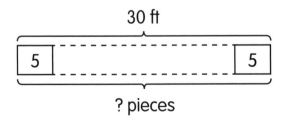

30 ft

5 | 5

? pieces

She cuts the string into _____ pieces.

Tell whether you need to multiply or divide.
Then solve.
Draw bar models to help you.

4. A strip of paper is 40 centimeters long.
It is cut into 4 equal pieces.
How long is each piece?

Each piece is _____ centimeters long.

5. Sara is making curtains.
She needs 5 meters of cloth for each curtain.
She has 45 meters of cloth.
How many curtains can she make?

She can make _____ curtains.

Tell whether you need to multiply or divide.
Then solve.
Use bar models to help you.

6.   The mass of 5 bags of potatoes is 30 kilograms.
     Each bag has the same mass.
     What is the mass of each bag?

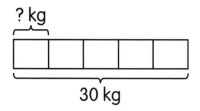

     The mass of each bag is _____ kilograms.

7.   There are 6 bricks.
     Each brick has a mass of 3 kilograms.
     What is the total mass of the 6 bricks?

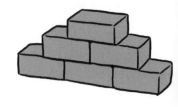

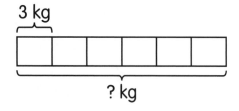

     The total mass of the 6 bricks is _____ kilograms.

Name: _____ Date: _____

Tell whether you need to multiply or divide.
Then solve.
Draw bar models to help you.

8. A pencil sharpener has a mass of 10 grams.
What is the total mass of 7 pencil sharpeners?

The total mass of 7 pencil sharpeners is _____ grams.

9. The total mass of 3 bags of flour is 6 kilograms.
Each bag has the same mass.
What is the mass of each bag of flour?

The mass of each bag of flour is _____ kilograms.

Tell whether you need to multiply or divide.
Then solve.
Draw bar models to help you.

10. 32 kilograms of rice is divided equally into some bags.
Each bag has a mass of 8 kilograms.
How many bags of rice are there?

There are _____ bags of rice.

11. Mrs. Evan's family drinks 5 liters of milk in a week.
How many liters of milk does her family drink in 7 weeks?

Her family drinks _____ liters of milk in 7 weeks.

Tell whether you need to multiply or divide.
Then solve.
Draw bar models to help you.

12.   Alberto pours 18 liters of water equally into 3 tanks.
How much water is there in each tank?

There are _____ liters of water in each tank.

13.   Barry collects 16 liters of water from a well.
He pours the water into some pails.
Each pail contains 4 liters of water.
How many pails are there in all?

There are _____ pails in all.

Tell whether you need to multiply or divide.
Then solve.
Draw bar models to help you.

14. Mariam gives $40 to her grandchildren.
Each of them gets $5.
How many grandchildren does she have?

She has _____ grandchildren.

15. Mrs. Tan buys 4 bottles of sauce.
Each bottle costs $4.
How much does she pay?

She pays $_____.

16. Linda has $50.
She spends all of it on some bags.
Each bag costs $10.
How many bags are there in all?

There are _____ bags in all.

Put On Your Thinking Cap!

Challenging Practice

Macy has some ropes, each 2 feet long.
Nellie has some ropes, each 3 feet long.
Oscar has some ropes, each 5 feet long.
What is the length of each line of ropes when they are of the same length?

Put On Your Thinking Cap!

Problem Solving

Sheena bakes 100 muffins.
She shares them equally with 4 other girls.
How many muffins does each girl get?
How many more muffins are needed so that each one
gets two more muffins?

Chapter Review/Test

Concepts and Skills

Match each bar model to a word problem.
Then solve the problem.

1.

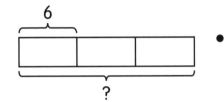

•   •

Ken has 18 strawberries. He divides them equally into 3 baskets. How many strawberries are in each basket?

_____ strawberries in each basket

2.

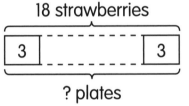

•   •

Ken has 18 strawberries. He puts 3 onto some plates. How many plates does he need?

_____ plates

3.

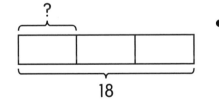

•   •

Ken has 3 plates. He puts 6 strawberries onto each plate. How many strawberries does he have in all?

_____ strawberries in all

Problem Solving

Write whether you need to multiply or divide.
Then solve.
Draw bar models to help you.

4.   Jason has 5 apricots on each tray.
He has a total of 50 apricots.
How many trays are there?

There are _____ trays.

5.   Claire paints 90 masks.
She divides the masks equally and puts them in baskets.
She puts 10 masks in each basket.
How many baskets are there in all?

There are _____ baskets in all.

Name: _____   Date: _____

Write whether you need to multiply or divide.
Then solve.
Draw bar models to help you.

6. Sonny helps his mother pack old books in 6 boxes.
       Each box has a mass of 4 kilograms.
       What is the total mass of 6 boxes of books?

The total mass of 6 boxes of books is _____ kilograms.

7. Sarah is making necklaces for her friends.
       She needs 12 feet of string for the necklaces.
       Each necklace needs a string 2 feet long.
       How many necklaces is Sarah making?

Sarah is making _____ necklaces.

Tell whether you need to multiply or divide.
Then solve.
Draw bar models to help you.

8.   Billy's cats drink 4 liters of milk in a week.
     How much milk do the cats drink in 4 weeks?

     The cats drink _____ liters of milk.

9.   Mr. Andres has 4 grandsons.
     He gives each of them $5.
     How much does he give his grandsons in all?

     He gives $_____ to his grandsons.

CHAPTER 17 Graphs and Line Plots

Practice 1 Reading Picture Graphs with Scales

Fill in the blanks. Use the picture graph to help you.

The picture graph shows the food a team ate after a softball game.

Food Eaten After the Game

Hot dogs	🍱 🍱 🍱
Salad	🍱 🍱 🍱 🍱
Oranges	🍱 🍱
Carrots	🍱 🍱 🍱
Apples	🍱 🍱

Key: Each 🍱 stands for 2 helpings of food.

--- Example ---

They had ___6___ helpings of hot dogs.

1. They had the same number of helpings of _____ as hot dogs.

2. They had _____ more helpings of salad than apples.

3. They had _____ helpings of salad and apples in all.

Jane and her classmates chose their favorite fairy tale character. This picture graph shows their choices.

Favorite Fairy Tale Characters

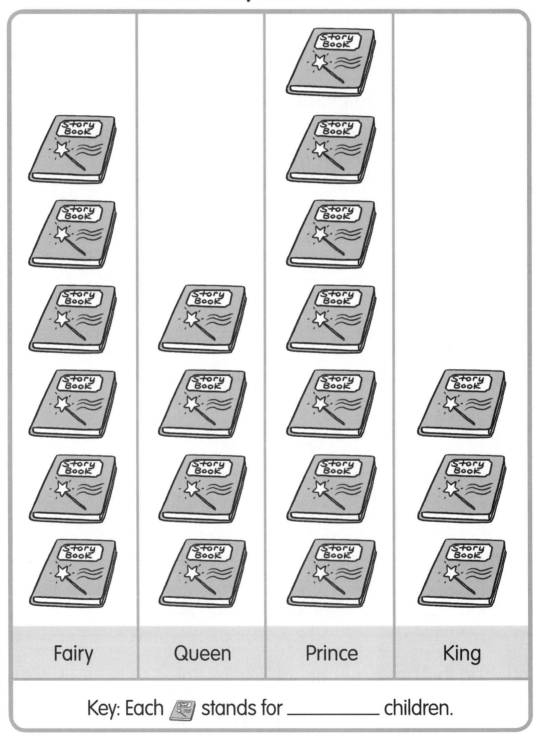

Key: Each 📖 stands for _____ children.

Name: _____   Date: _____

Fill in the blanks.
Use the picture graph on page 182 to help you.

Example ─────────────────────────────────────

How many characters are shown?

_____4_____

---

4. Which is the most common favorite character?

_____

5. Which is the least common favorite character?

_____

6. 8 children like the Queen.
What does each 📖 stand for?

_____

7. How many children chose the Prince?

_____ children

8. How many more children chose the Fairy than the Queen
as their favorite character?

_____ more children

9. The total number of children who chose _____

or _____ as their favorite character is the same as the
number of children who chose the Prince.

Fill in the blanks.
Use the picture graph to help you.

Randy's home is near a School, a Bus Stop, a Store, and a Post Office.
He draws a picture graph to show how far his home is from these places.

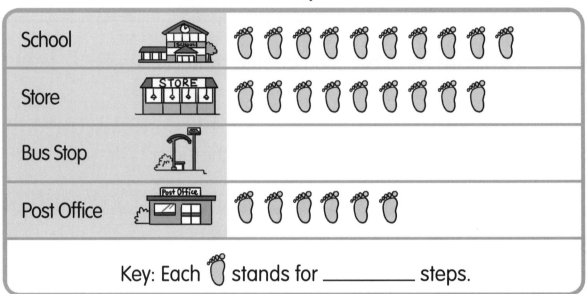

Number of Steps from Home

Key: Each 🦶 stands for _____ steps.

Example

The School is 100 steps from Randy's home.

Each 🦶 stands for ___*10*___ steps.

---

10.   The Store is _____ steps from Randy's home.

11.   Randy's home is 50 steps from the Bus Stop.

He will draw _____ 🦶 on the graph.

12.   The Post Office is 80 steps from Randy's home.

He will draw _____ more 🦶 on the graph.

Practice 2   Making Picture Graphs

1.   Count the boxes of fruit juice on the shelves.
     Complete the tally chart.

Fruit Juice	Tally	Number of Boxes of Fruit Juice
Apple	☰☰ ☰☰ ☰☰ ☰☰	
Orange		
Pear		
Grape		

2. **Fill in the missing numbers.**

Fruit Juice	Apple	Orange	Pear	Grape
Number of Boxes of Fruit Juice	20			

3. **Then complete the graph.**

Number of Boxes of Fruit Juice

Key: Each ☐ stands for 2 boxes of fruit juice.

Fill in the blanks.

4. There are _____ boxes of apple juice.

5. There are _____ boxes of fruit juice in all.

6. Look at the picture.
Count the animals in the picture.
Then complete the tally chart.

Animals	Tally	Number of Animals
🐱		
🐦		
🐰		
🐹		

7. Use the picture and your answer on page 187. Show the number of animals by coloring the 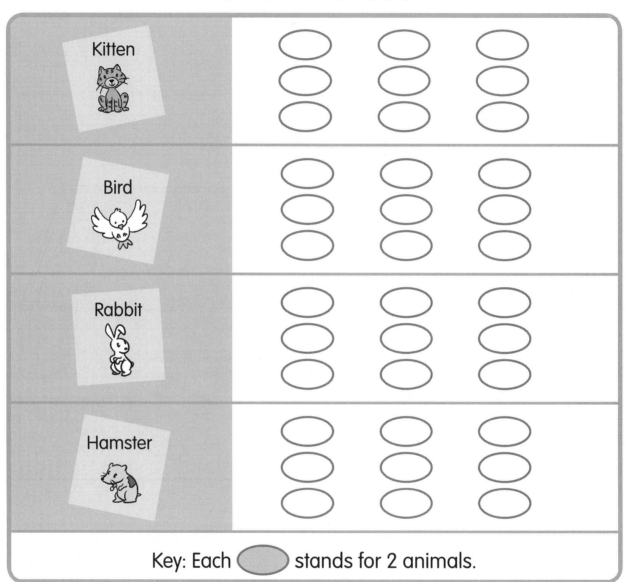 in the graph.

Animals in the Picture

8. **These are five kinds of stickers Amy has.**
   Count the number of stickers and complete the tally chart.

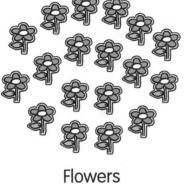

Flowers

Seashells

Puppies

Hearts

Stars

Stickers	Tally	Number of Stickers
Flower 🌼		
Puppy 🐶		
Heart 💗		
Star ⭐		
Seashell 🐚		

Now fill in the blanks.

9. Amy's stickers show _____ flowers, _____ seashells, _____ puppies, _____ hearts, and _____ stars.

10. Then complete the picture graph. Give it a title.

Title: _____

Seashell	
Puppy	
Star	⬭ ⬭ ⬭ ⬭ ⬭ ⬭ ⬭ ⬭ ⬭ ⬭
Flower	
Heart	

Key: Each ⬭ stands for 3 stickers.

Look at the pictures.
Then fill in the blanks.

Peter, Roy, Shantel, and Amy are friends.
They made up a story that takes place in outer space.
Each drew pictures of his or her favorite thing for the story.

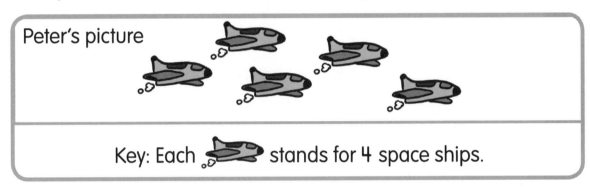

Peter's picture

Key: Each 🚀 stands for 4 space ships.

11.   Peter drew _____ pictures for the story.

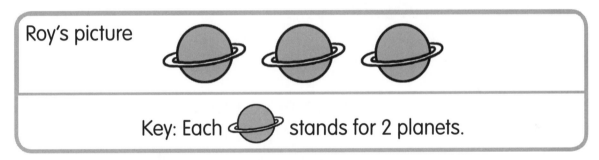

Roy's picture

Key: Each 🪐 stands for 2 planets.

12.   Roy drew _____ pictures for the story.

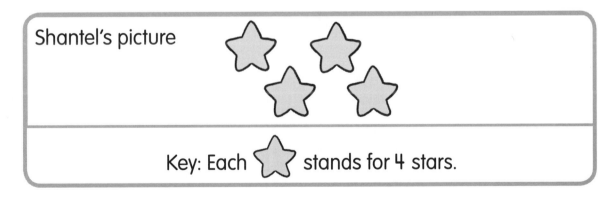

Shantel's picture

Key: Each ⭐ stands for 4 stars.

13.   Shantel drew _____ pictures for the story.

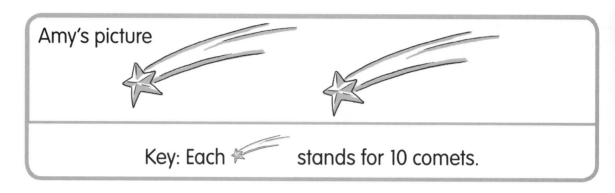

Amy's picture

Key: Each ⭐ stands for 10 comets.

14. Amy drew _____ pictures for the story.

15. Complete.

Kinds of Things in the Story	🚀	🪐	⭐	☄️
Number of Favorite Things				

Use the data in the table to complete the picture graph.
Choose a symbol to show the things in the story.
Put a key under the graph. Then give the graph a title.

Title: _____

🚀	🪐	☆	☄️

Key: Each _____ stands for 2 things in the story.

Practice 3   Real-World Problems: Picture Graphs

Use the picture graph to answer the questions.

Dora and her friends compare their sticker collections.
She draws a picture graph to show the number of stickers they have.
However, she accidentally spills her drink on part of the graph.

Number of Stickers

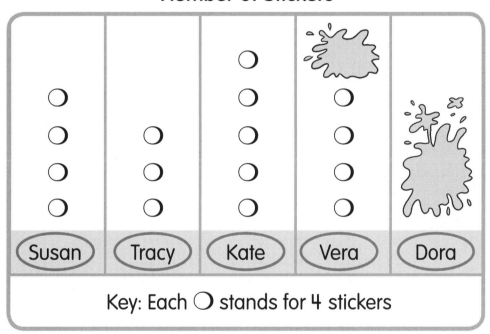

Key: Each ○ stands for 4 stickers

1.   How many stickers does Susan have? _____

2.   How many more stickers does Kate have than Tracy? _____

3.   Dora has 8 stickers.

     How many ○ should there be on the graph? _____

4.   Vera has 24 stickers.
     How many more ○ must be on the graph? _____

5.   How many stickers do Susan and Tracy have in all? _____

The graph shows the number of children playing each game at a fair.

Number of Children Playing Games

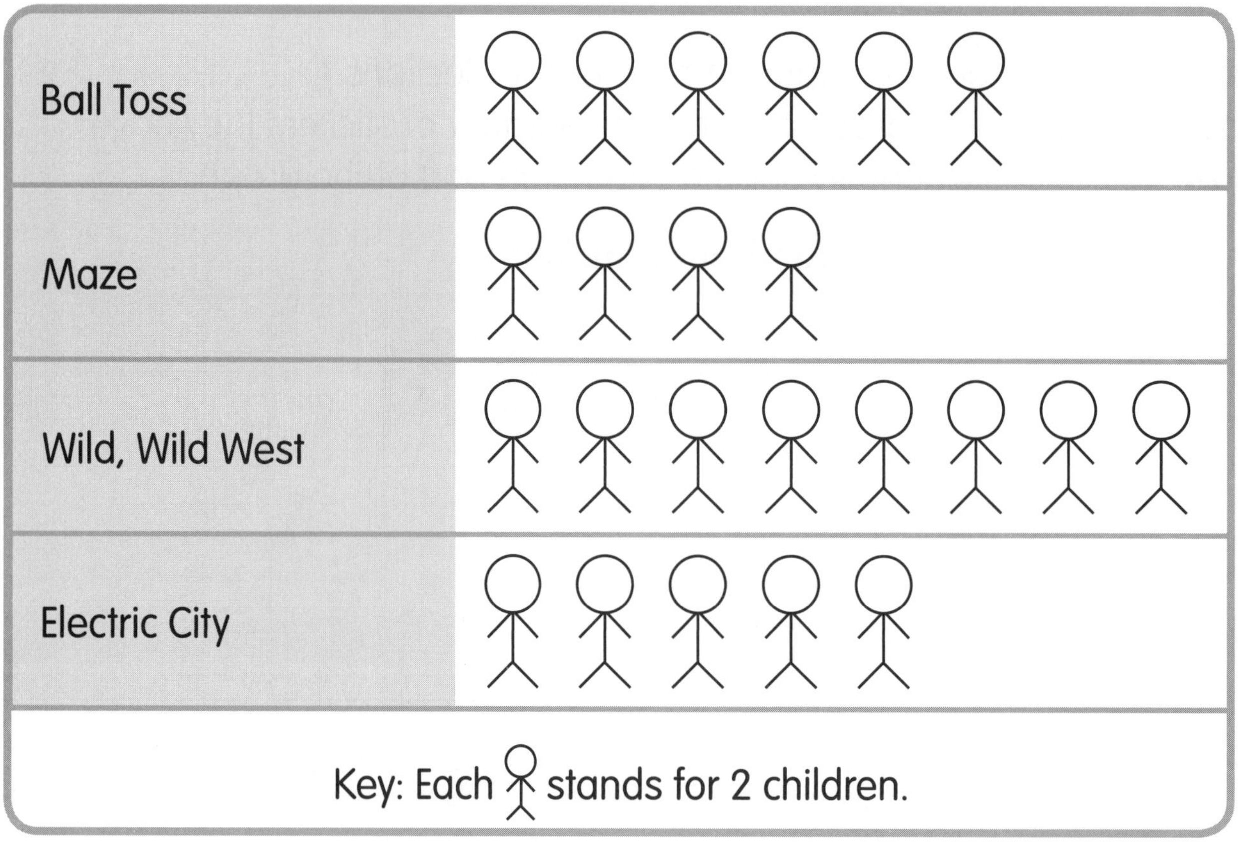

Ball Toss	🧍 🧍 🧍 🧍 🧍 🧍
Maze	🧍 🧍 🧍 🧍
Wild, Wild West	🧍 🧍 🧍 🧍 🧍 🧍 🧍 🧍 🧍
Electric City	🧍 🧍 🧍 🧍 🧍

Key: Each 🧍 stands for 2 children.

Use the picture graph to answer the questions.

6. There are 6 boys at the Electric City stall.
How many girls are at the Electric City stall? _____

7. 6 of the children who play Wild, Wild West are girls.

How many are boys? _____

8. 2 girls are at the Maze.
4 boys are at the Ball Toss.
How many girls are at the Maze or Ball Toss in all? _____

9. Abigail visits a pet store and sees different kinds of fish.
Use the data given to finish the graph.

Use a 🐟 to stand for 4 fish.

  a. There are 16 clown fish.

  b. There are 12 more barb fish than clown fish.

  c. There are 4 more goldfish than barb fish.

  d. There are 8 fewer guppies than goldfish.

  e. There are the same number of discus fish as clown
    fish and guppies together.

Fishes in a Pet Store

Goldfish	Guppy	Clown fish	Discus fish	Barb fish

Key: Each _____ stands for 4 fish.

10. Gita made banana muffins for her family.
Use the data given to complete the graph.

Use △ to stand for 2 cups.

a. Gita used 2 cups of sugar.
She used the same number of cups of oil.

b. She used 4 cups of milk.
She used 2 more cups of oatmeal than the number of cups of milk.

c. She used 6 cups of mashed bananas.

Banana Muffin Ingredients

Oatmeal	
Sugar	
Oil	
Milk	
Mashed Bananas	

Key: Each _____ stands for 2 cups.

Name: ______________________________ Date: ____________________

Practice 4 Bar Graphs and Line Plots

Ms. Rafael's students took a Science quiz.
Each student answered 10 questions.
Each correct answer earned 1 point.
The tally chart below shows the scores.

Complete.

1. Complete the tally chart.

Scores	Tally	Number of Students
1		
2		
3	////	
4	/	
5	///	
6	~~////~~	
7	~~////~~ /	
8	//	
9	/	
10	///	

2. Complete the bar graph to show the data.
Label your graph.

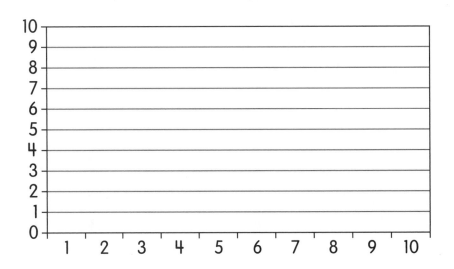

3. Use the data in the bar graph to create a line plot.

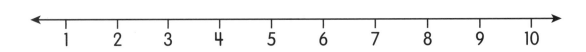

Use the bar graph or line plot to answer the questions.

4. How many students scored 6 points? _____ students

5. How many students scored more than 5 points? _____ students

6. How many students took the Science quiz? _____ students

7. Ms. Rafael awarded a sticker to each student who scored more than
7 points.

How many stickers did she give out? _____ stickers

Put On Your Thinking Cap!
Challenging Practice

Tricia read a story book.
She recorded the number of pages she read every day for 3 days.
She drew a ☐ for every 2 pages she read.

		☐	
		☐	
	☐	☐	
☐	☐	☐	
1st day	2nd day	3rd day	4th day

Key: Each ☐ stands for 2 pages.

The number of pages Tricia read follows a pattern.
If this pattern continues, how many pages will Tricia read on the 4th day?

Tricia will read _____ pages on the 4th day.

Put On Your Thinking Cap!

Problem Solving

The graph shows the number of points 5 children scored on a science test.
The total score for the test is 40.
Complete the graph using the information given.

Ariel scored all the points she could.
Tyrone scored 8 points less than Ariel.
Nicole and Vera had the same number of points.

Points Scored on a Science Test

Ariel	
Edwin	✓ ✓ ✓ ✓ ✓ ✓ ✓
Nicole	
Vera	✓ ✓ ✓ ✓ ✓ ✓ ✓ ✓ ✓
Tyrone	

Each ✓ stands for 4 points.

Chapter Review/Test

Vocabulary

Fill in the blanks with words from the box.

key
picture graph
tally chart

1. The _____ shows what a picture or symbol stands for.

2. A _____ shows data using pictures or symbols.

3. You record the number of things in a _____.

Concepts and Skills

4. Tammy went to a bird park.
Help her make a tally chart of the birds she saw on page 202.

Tally Chart

Birds	Tally	Number of birds

5. Then complete the picture graph of the data in exercise 4. Give it a title.

Title: _____

Jay	Swallow	Robin	Flamingo	Peacock

Key: Each ○ stands for 3 birds.

Name: _____   Date: _____

The graph shows how much money each child has saved in a month.

Money Saved in One Month

Key: Each 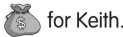 stands for $2.

Use the graph to find the missing numbers.

6. How much has Keith saved?

There are _____  for Keith.

_____ × $_____ = $_____.

Keith has saved $_____

7. How much have Michelle and Alberto saved in all? _____

There are 7  for Michelle.

_____ × $_____ = $_____

There are 6  for Alberto.

_____ × $_____ = $_____

$ _____ + $_____ = $_____

Michelle and Alberto saved $_____ in all.

8. How much more has Michelle saved than Gloria?

There are 7 🛍️ for Michelle.

_____ × $_____ = $_____

There are 5 🛍️ for Gloria.

_____ × $_____ = $_____

$_____ – $_____ = $_____

Michelle has saved $_____ more than Gloria.

9. Grace has 2 🛍️.

How much less has she saved than Gloria?

_____ × $_____ = $_____

$_____ – $_____ = $_____

Grace has saved $_____ less than Gloria.

The chart shows the number of beads that each child used to make a bracelet.

	Number of beads
Andrea	9
Abby	7
Zoe	7
Lorie	5
Bob	8
Mike	4
Shelly	7
Angel	6

Use the data to complete the bar graph below.
Give your graph a title.

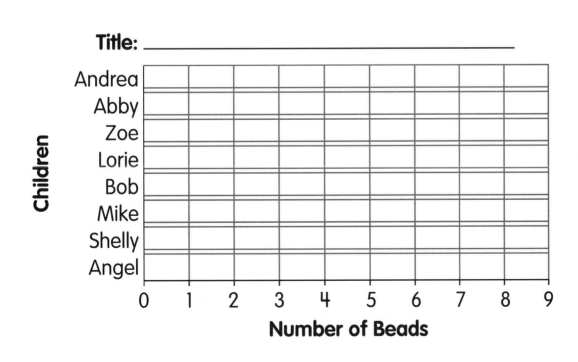

Make a line plot using the data on the bar graph on page 205. Then answer the questions.

10. How many children used 6 beads? _____

11. How many children used fewer than 7 beads? _____

12. How many children made bracelets? _____

13. How many children used more than 7 beads? _____

14. How many beads did the children use in all? _____

Cumulative Review

for Chapters 15 to 17

Concepts and Skills

Skip-count.

1. 3, 6, 9, _____, _____, _____, _____, _____,

_____, _____

2. 4, 8, 12, _____, _____, _____, _____, _____,

_____, _____

Fill in the blanks.

3. 4 groups of 3 = _____ × _____ = _____

4. 8 groups of 3 = _____ × _____ = _____

5. 3 groups of 4 = _____ × _____ = _____

6. 9 groups of 4 = _____ × _____ = _____

Use dot paper to find the missing numbers.

7.

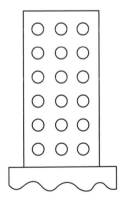   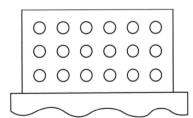

_____ × 3 = _____   _____ × _____ = _____

8.

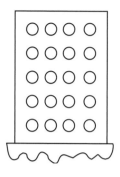   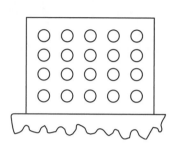

_____ × _____ = _____   _____ × _____ = _____

Complete the multiplication sentences.
Use dot paper to help you.

9. 9 × 3 = _____   **10.** 7 × 3 = _____

   3 × 9 = _____   3 × 7 = _____

11. 10 × 4 = _____   **12.** 6 × 4 = _____

   4 × 10 = _____   4 × 6 = _____

Fill in the blanks.

13. 10 × 4 = _____   7 × 4 = 10 groups of 4 − 3 groups of 4

                              = _____ − 12

                              = _____

14. 5 × 3 = _____   7 × 3 = 5 groups of 3 + 2 groups of 3

                              = _____ + 6

                              = _____

Complete the multiplication and division sentences.

15. _____ × 3 = 15   15 ÷ 3 = _____

16. _____ × 4 = 20   20 ÷ 4 = _____

Fill in the blanks.
Use the picture graphs to help you.

A large bottle contains different kinds of nuts.
The graph shows the number of each kind of nut in the jar.

Kinds of Nuts in a Jar

Almond	◯ ◯ ◯ ◯ ◯ ◯
Peanut	◯ ◯ ◯ ◯ ◯ ◯ ◯ ◯ ◯ ◯
Cashew	◯ ◯ ◯ ◯
Walnut	◯ ◯ ◯
Pecan	◯ ◯ ◯ ◯

Key: Each ◯ stands for 2 nuts.

17.   There are _____ peanuts in the jar.

18.   The number of _____ and _____ in the jar is the same.

19.   There are _____ fewer walnuts than almonds.

20.   There are _____ more peanuts than cashews.

21.   There are _____ almonds and pecans in all.

Count the vegetables in a bin.
Then complete the tally chart.

Vegetable	Tally
Onion	
Cabbage	
Carrot	
Potato	
Tomato	

22. Use the picture and the tally chart to make a bar graph.

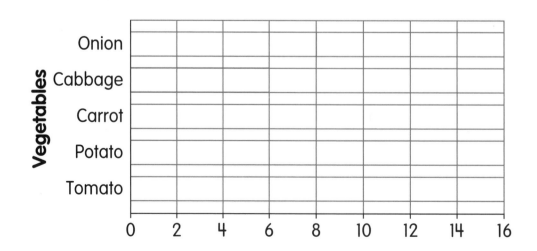

Complete.
Use your bar graph to help you.

23. How many carrots are there? _____

24. How many tomatoes are there? _____

25. How many cabbages are there? _____

Problem Solving
Solve.
Draw bar models to help you.

26. Alicia has 3 bags.
She puts 10 beads in each bag.
How many beads does she have?

There are _____ beads in all.

Solve.

Draw bar models to help you.

27.   Peter has 18 crayons.
He divides them into 3 equal groups.
How many crayons are in each group?

There are _____ crayons in each group.

28.   Yasmin buys 30 stickers.
She distributes the stickers equally among her 5 friends.
How many stickers does each of her friends get?

Each friend gets _____ stickers.

29.   A day camp has 12 soccer balls.
Each team uses 3 balls.
How many teams are there?

There are _____ teams.

30. 5 bags of food for a food drive have a mass of 25 kilograms.
Each bag has the same mass.
What is the mass of each bag?

The mass of each bag is _____ kilograms.

31. The total length of a piece of lace is 28 feet.
It is cut into equal pieces 4 feet long.
How many pieces are there?

There are _____ pieces.

32. Andrew uses 6 liters of water to water his plants every day.
How many liters of water does he use in 4 days?

He uses _____ liters of water.

Complete the picture graph using Exercises 33 and 34.
Then use the graph to solve Exercises 35 and 36.
A group of people attended a workshop.
They were divided into 5 groups.
The number of people in each group is shown in the graph.

Groups at the Workshop

Group 1	☺☺☺☺☺☺☺
Group 2	☺☺☺
Group 3	☺☺☺☺☺☺
Group 4	☺☺☺☺☺
Group 5	
Key: Each ☺ stands for _____ people.	

33. There were 15 people in Group 2.

What does each ☺ stand for? _____

34. Draw ☺ to show 20 people in Group 5.

35. 7 people in Group 3 were women.

How many were men? _____

36. There were 50 men in Group 1 and Group 4. How many women were there in Group 1 and Group 4?

_____

CHAPTER 18 Lines and Surfaces

Practice 1   Parts of Lines and Curves
Trace the correct figures.

1. Parts of lines only

2. Curves only

3. Parts of lines and curves

Look at these letters.

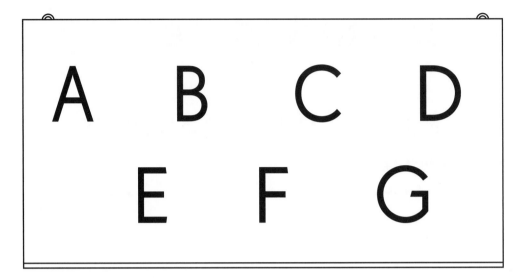

Which of these letters have

4. parts of lines only? _____

5. curves only? _____

6. parts of lines and curves? _____

Draw three other letters using parts of lines only.

7.

Draw three other letters using parts of lines and curves.

8.

J P

**Julie drew pictures with parts of lines and curves.
Count the parts of lines and curves she used.**

Example

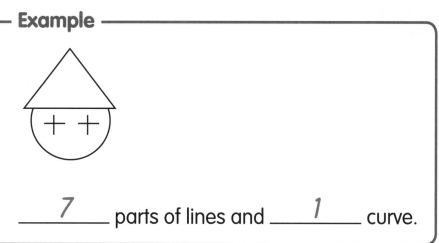

_____7_____ parts of lines and _____1_____ curve.

9.

_____ parts of lines and _____ curves.

10.

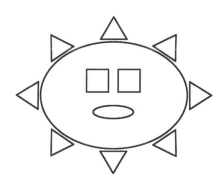

_____ parts of lines and _____ curves.

Count the number of parts of lines in each figure.
Count the number of curves.
Sort the figures into two groups.
Sort using the numbers of parts of lines and curves.
Color each group a different color.

11.

Draw a picture with

12. more than 5 parts of lines.

13. fewer than 8 curves.

14. more than 10 parts of lines and curves.

 **Math Journal**

Draw a happy face using curves only.

Draw a sad face using parts of lines and curves.

Practice 2   Flat and Curved Surfaces

Look at the objects.
Then fill in the blanks.

┌─ Example ───┐

An orange has _____0_____ flat surfaces.

_____1_____ curved surface.

└──┘

1.

A can has _____ flat surfaces.

_____ curved surface.

2.

A plastic cup has _____ flat surface.

_____ curved surface.

3.

The cereal box has _____ flat surfaces.

_____ curved surfaces.

Look around your home.
Find two objects that have only flat surfaces.
Name and draw them.

4. _____

5. _____

6. **Circle the solids that you can stack.**

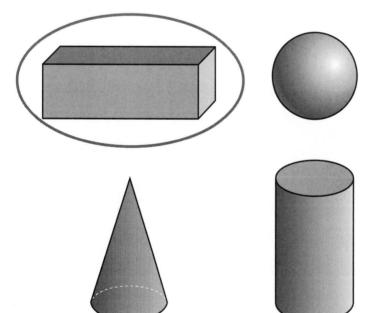

7. **Circle the solids that you can roll.**

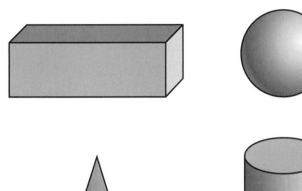
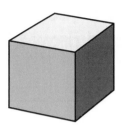

8. **Circle the solids that you can slide.**

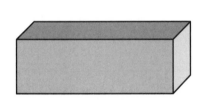

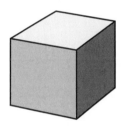

Look around your home.
Find two objects that have only curved surfaces.
Name and draw them.

9. _____

10. _____

Name: _____ Date: _____

How many flat and curved surfaces does each object have? Write your answers in the table.

tissue box

egg

piece of paper

basketball

library card

cereal box

vase

11.	0 flat surfaces	
12.	1 flat surface	
13.	1 curved surface	
14.	2 flat surfaces	
15.	6 flat surfaces	

Cut out pictures of objects in newspapers or magazines.
Paste them here.
Count the flat and curved surfaces in each object.
Write your answers next to the picture.

16.

Put On Your Thinking Cap!

Challenging Practice

The shapes at the bottom of this page can be combined to make a square.

Color the pieces yellow.

Cut them out and paste them below to make the square.

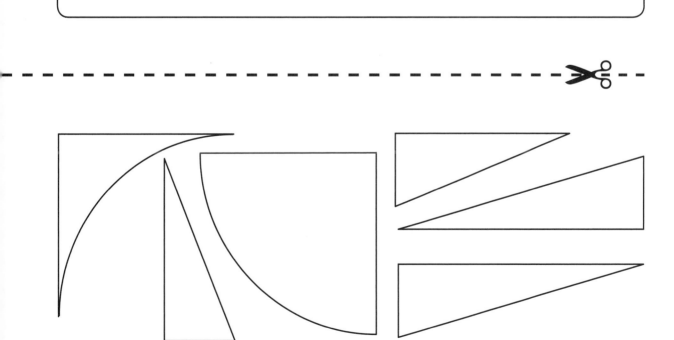

Chapter Review/Test

Vocabulary
Fill in the blanks with words from the box.

curved	stack	roll	flat

1.   A ball has a _____ surface.

It can _____ on the ground.

2.   A picture has a _____ surface.

You can _____ pictures on top of each other.

Concepts and Skills

Circle the correct answer.

3.

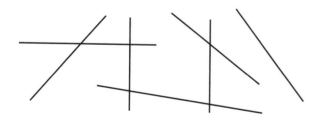

These are (parts of lines, curves).

4.

These are (parts of lines, curves).

Draw.

5. A figure that has five parts of lines and three curves	**6.** A figure that has only parts of lines
7. An object that has only curved surfaces	**8.** An object that has two flat surfaces and one curved surface

Problem Solving

Each pattern is made of curves and straight lines.
Find the pattern.
Then complete the pattern.

9.

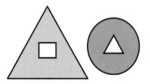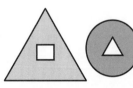 _____

CHAPTER 19 Shapes and Patterns

Practice 1 Plane Shapes

Look at the shapes.

1. Color the circles green, the triangles yellow, the rectangles purple, the trapezoids blue, the hexagons red, and the pentagons orange.

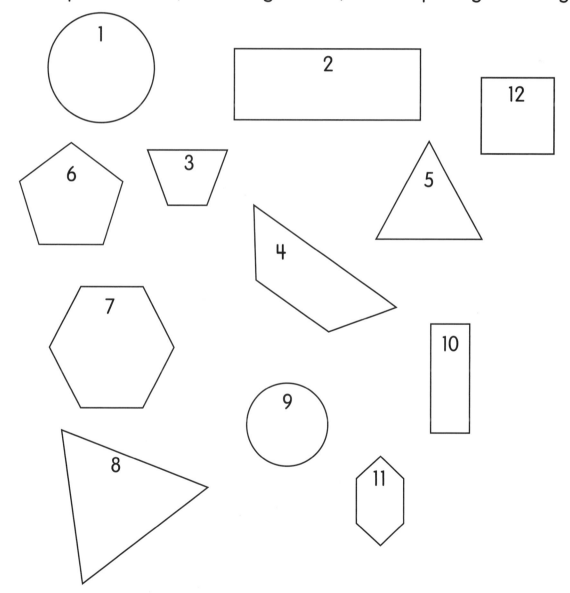

2. Which of these are quadrilaterals? Write the numbers: _____

Draw lines on each shape to show the smaller shapes.

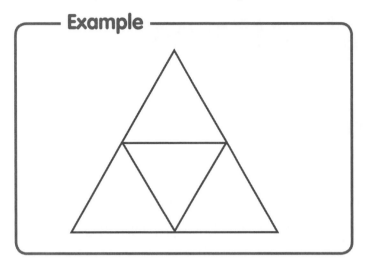

2.

3.

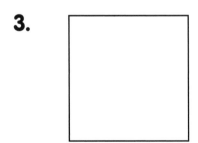

4. **Cut out the shapes.**
Then glue them on top of the shape given.
Here are two simple rules to follow:
a) All cut-outs must be used.
b) Cut-outs cannot overlap.

Plane Shape	Cut-outs

5.   Draw lines on each figure to show how it is made with these shapes: triangle, square, rectangle, trapezoid, hexagon, and pentagon.

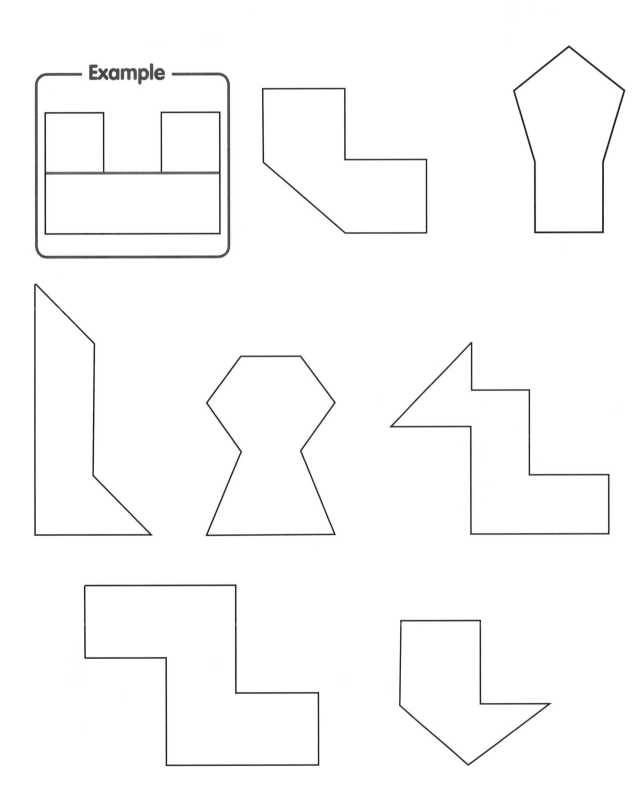

Each figure is made with two shapes.
Name the shapes.

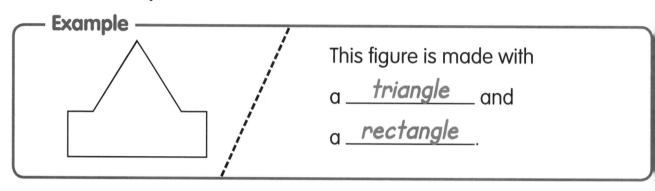

Example

This figure is made with

a ___triangle___ and

a ___rectangle___.

6.

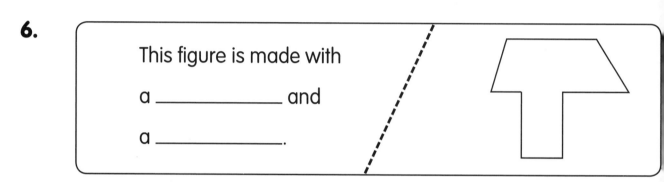

This figure is made with

a _____ and

a _____.

7.

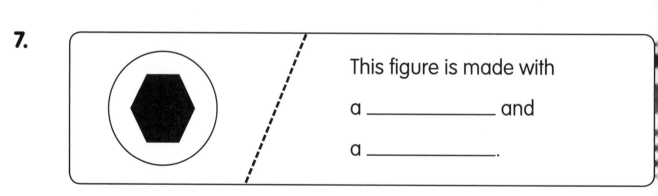

This figure is made with

a _____ and

a _____.

8.

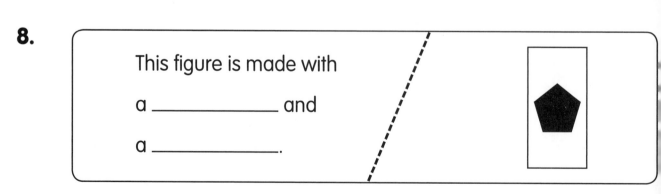

This figure is made with

a _____ and

a _____.

Name: _____ Date: _____

A part is missing from each figure.
Color the shape that makes the figure complete.

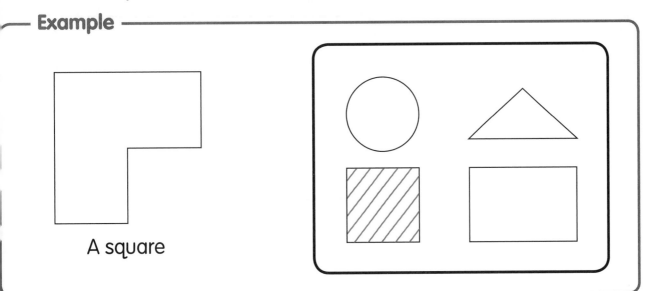

A square

9.

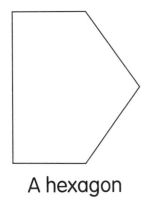

A hexagon

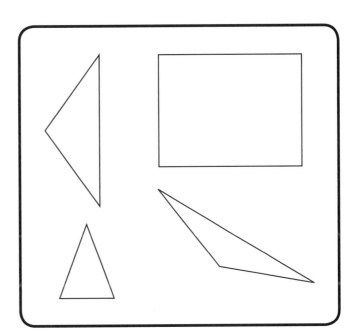

A part is missing from each figure.
Color the shape that makes the figure complete.

10.

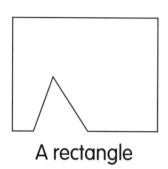

A rectangle

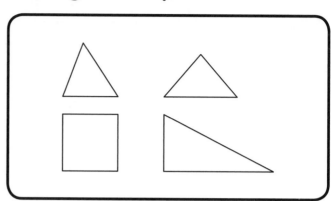

11.

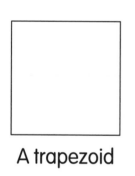

A trapezoid

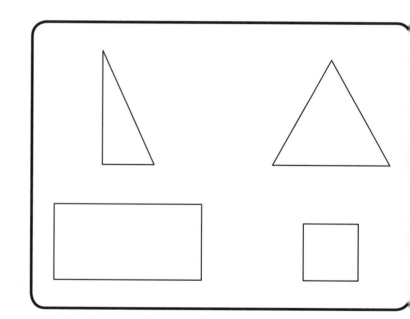

12.

A pentagon

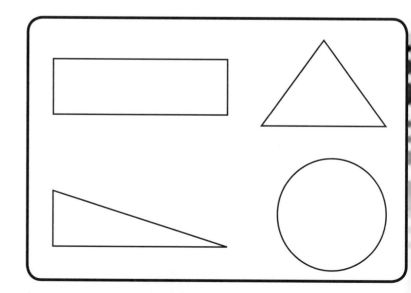

13.   Cut out the shapes.
Then glue them on top of the figure.

Here are two simple rules to follow.
(a) All cut-outs must be used.
(b) Cut-outs cannot overlap.

Figure	Cut-outs ✂

Figure	Cut-outs ✂

opy each figure.

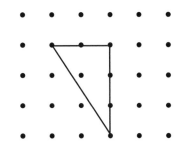

13.

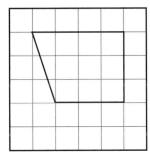

Copy each figure.

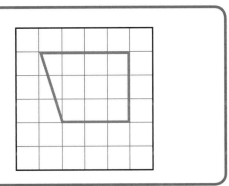

14.

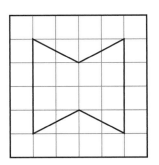   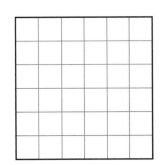

Draw a quadrilateral on the dot grid paper.
Circle the angles.
Write how many angles.

15.

Draw a shape with three angles on the dot grid paper.

16.

Practice 2 Solid Shapes

Write the number of solid shapes used in each model.

1.

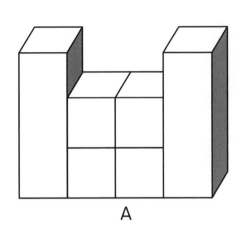

A

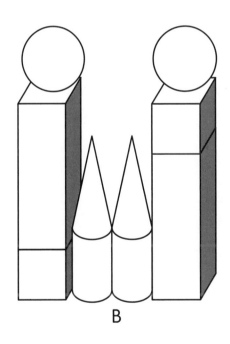

B

Object	A	B
Rectangular prism	2	2
Cube		
Cone		
Cylinder		
Sphere		

Look at the cube.

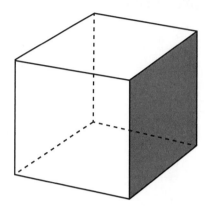

2. How many faces can you see on the cube?

3. What do you notice about the faces on the cube?

4. Name some objects in your classroom or home that are cubes.

Practice 3   Making Patterns

Look at the pattern.
Draw what comes next.

Example

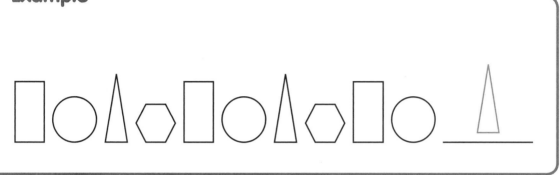

1.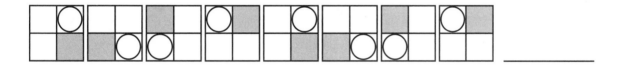

2.

3.   _____

Circle the correct shapes or figures made of shapes to complete the pattern.

Example

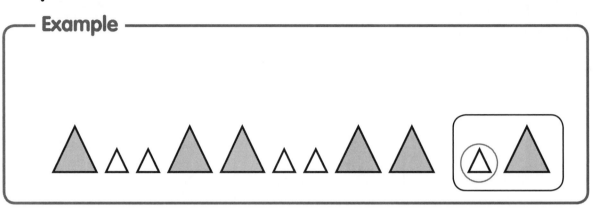

4.

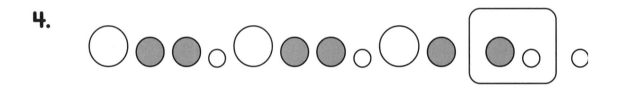

5.

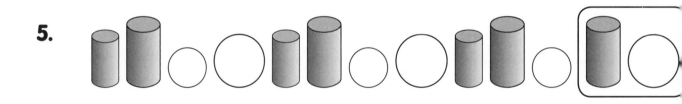

6.

7.

Circle the correct shapes or figures made of shapes to complete the pattern.

8.

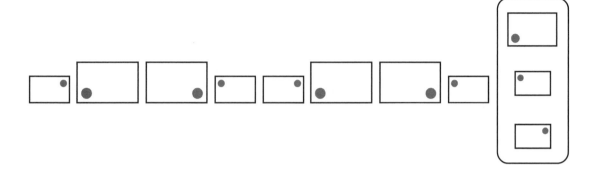

9.

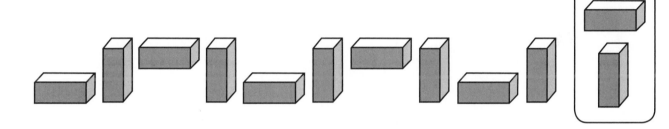

10.

Circle the correct shapes or figures made of shapes to complete the pattern.

11.

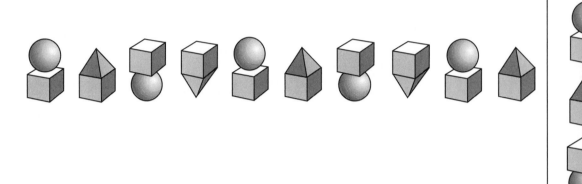

12.

13.

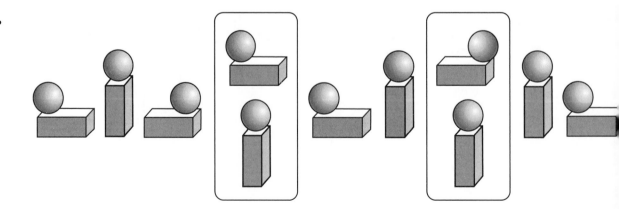

Math Journal

This pattern is made with plane shapes.
Circle the mistake in the pattern.
Name the correct shape.
Then draw the repeating pattern unit.

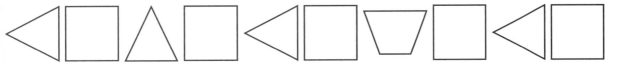

The correct plane shape is a _____.

This pattern is made with solid shapes.
Circle the mistake in the pattern.
Write what the correct shape is.
Then draw or describe the repeating unit.

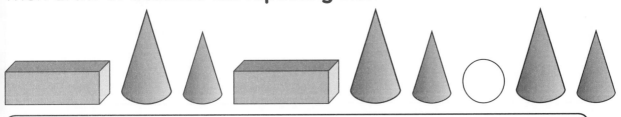

The correct solid shape is a _____.

Use plane shapes to make a pattern

1.   using shapes of different types.

2.   using the same shape of different colors.

3.   by turning the shape.

Chapter Review/Test

Vocabulary
Fill in the blanks with words from the box.

hexagon
trapezoid
pattern
turning

1. You can form a repeating _____ using

   different shapes, colors, sizes, and

   by _____ the shapes.

2. A _____ has six sides.

3. A _____ is four-sided like the square and the rectangle.

Concepts and Skills
Match the shape to its name.

4.

   _____

5.

   _____

6.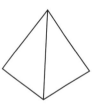

   _____

7.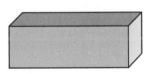

   _____

8.

   _____

9.

   _____

a. pentagon   b. cylinder   c. hexagon

d. pyramid   e. rectangular prism   f. trapezoid

Use this shape to make another bigger shape.
Write how many of this shape you used.
Name the shape you made.

10.

Draw lines to separate this rectangle into several copies of the same smaller shape.

11.

Copy the shape onto the dot grid.
Circle one of the angles of the shape.

12.

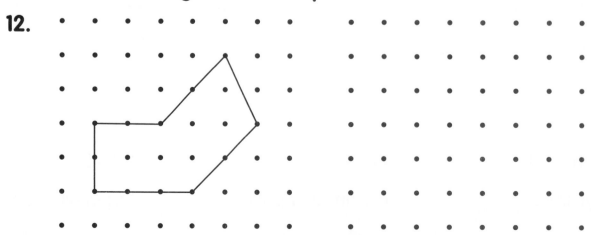

Write the number of plane shapes that make up this figure.

13.

Solid shape	How many?
Rectangle	
Triangle	

Write the number of solid shapes that make up this model.

14.

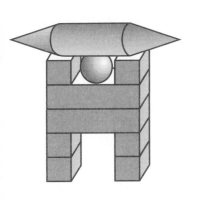

Solid shape	How many?
Cube	
Rectangular prism	
Cone	
Sphere	
Cylinder	

Draw the next figure in each pattern.

15.

16.

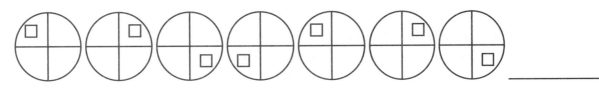

Complete the pattern.
Circle the correct solid or model.

17.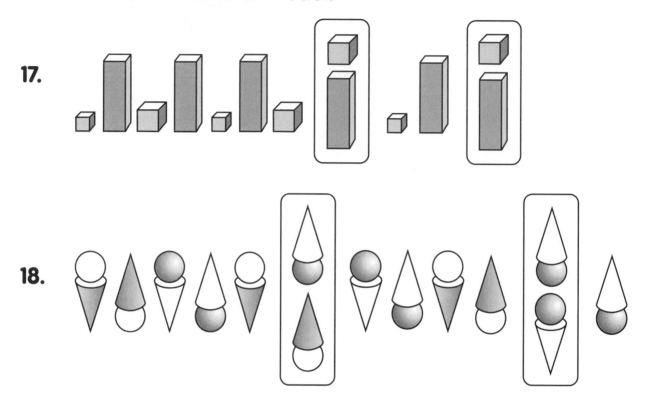

18.

Problem Solving

Look at the pattern.
Draw what comes next.

19.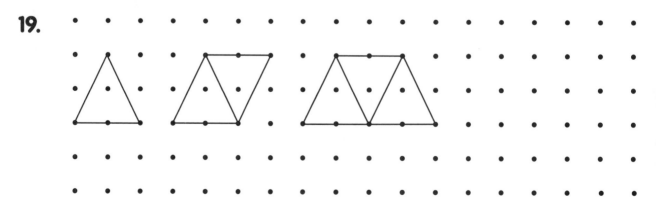

20. Susan wants to make a hexagon using the least number of one shape.
   a. Which can she use?
   b. How many of this shape will she use?

Name: _____ Date: _____

Cumulative Review

for Chapters 18 and 19

Concepts and Skills

Look at the letters.
Then fill in the blanks.

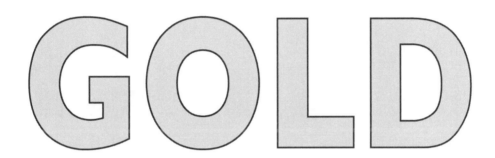

1. Letter G has _____ parts of lines and _____ curves.

2. Letter _____ has curves only.

3. Letters _____ and _____ have the most parts of lines.

4. The total number of curves in the first and last letters is _____.

5. The total number of parts of lines in all the letters is _____.

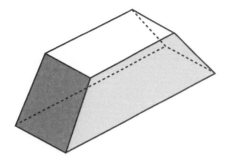

6. This solid has _____ faces. They have the shapes of a _____ and a _____.

7. This solid has _____ flat surfaces. Each surface has the shape of a _____.

Look at the drawings.
Count the number of curves and parts of lines in each.
Complete the table.

8.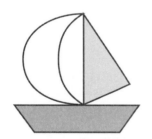

9.

10.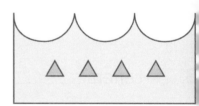

Drawing	Parts of Lines	Curves
8		
9		
10		

Name: _____ Date: _____

Draw dotted lines within each figure to show the shapes it is made of.

11.

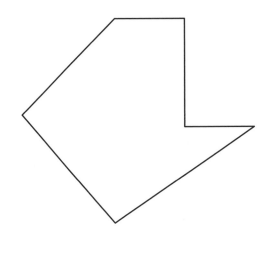

12.

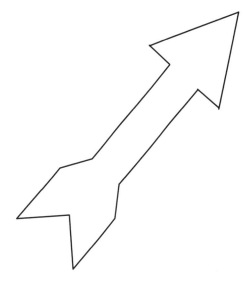

13.

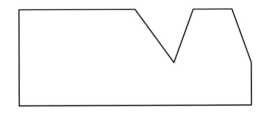

14.

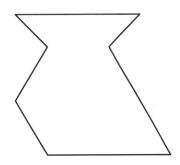

Look at the picture.
Count and write the number of shapes you see.

15.

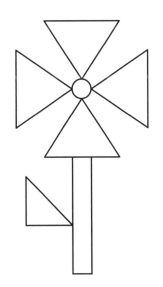

Shape	Number
Circle	
Triangle	
Rectangle	

Copy on dot grid paper.

16.

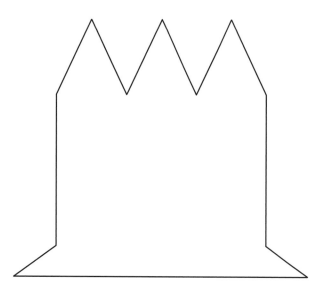

. . . .

. . . .

. . . .

. . . .

. . . .

. . . .

. . . .

. . . .

. . . .

Problem Solving.

Look at the pattern.
What comes next?
Fill in the blank.

17.

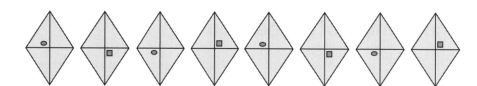

_____

Circle what comes next.

18.

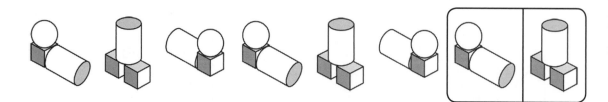

End-of-Year Review

Test Prep

Multiple Choice

Fill in the circle next to the correct answer.

1. Which of the following is correct?

    (A) In 345, the digit 3 is in the ones place.

    (B) In 345, the digit 5 is in the ones place.

    (C) In 345, the digit 5 is in the tens place.

    (D) In 345, the digit 4 is in the hundreds place.

2. What comes next? 5, 15, 25 _____.

    (A) 0   (B) 10   (C) 35   (D) 50

3. The sum of 500 and 43 is _____.

    (A) 345   (B) 354   (C) 435   (D) 543

4. Farmer Ben has 456 chickens.
He has 336 ducks.
What is the difference between the number of
chickens and ducks?

    (A) 130   (B) 120   (C) 576   (D) 932

5.

How many groups of 5 can you make?

    (A) 2   (B) 4   (C) 5   (D) 10

6. Rope A is 45 feet long.
Rope B is 71 feet long.
How much longer is Rope B than Rope A?

(A) 26 ft   (B) 34 ft   (C) 36 ft   (D) 116 ft

7. Roma weighs about _____ kilograms.

(A) 3 kg   (B) 442 kg   (C) 81 g   (D) 4300 g

8. $137 + 40 =$ _____.

(A) 177   (B) 187   (C) 237   (D) 277

9.

Which is the correct amount of money shown?

(A) $16.00   (B) $20.50   (C) $16.24   (D) $19.34

10. Angeline got home at 6:20 P.M.
Which clock shows the time Angeline got home?

(A)

(B)

(C)

(D)

11. Which has only flat surfaces?

(A) a banana

(B) a bottle

(C) a balloon

(D) a square box

12. Yumi buys a violin for $287.
She gives the cashier $300.
How much change does she get?

Ⓐ $20　　Ⓑ $17　　Ⓒ $23　　Ⓓ $13

13.

Zach makes some juice. How much does he make?

Ⓐ 1 L　　Ⓑ 10 L　　Ⓒ 5 L　　Ⓓ 12 L

14. Which is a part of a line?

Ⓐ 　　Ⓑ ╱　　Ⓒ 〜　　Ⓓ ⌒

15. Which is not divided into equal parts?

Ⓐ

Ⓑ

Ⓒ

Ⓓ

Short Answer

Read the questions carefully.
Write your answers in the space provided.

16. What is 345 + 70?   _____

17. ☆ stands for 4 people.

What does ☆ ☆ ☆ ☆ ☆ ☆ stand for? _____

18. What is 920 – 80?   _____

19. Write an odd number bigger than 80 but smaller
than 100. _____

20. How many parts of lines and curves are there?

_____ parts of lines

_____ curves

21. Joy and Andrew share a pie equally.
What fraction of the pie does Andrew eat?

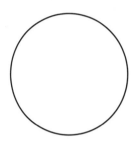

Andrew eats _____ of the pie.

22. Joe has $2.
He buys a toy for 75¢.
How much does he have left?
$_____

23. How many of each shape are there?

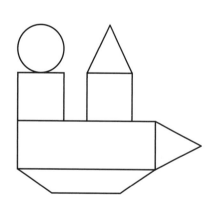

Shape	How many?
◯	
▢	
△	
▭	
⬡	

Fill in the blanks.

24. 789 = 7 hundreds _____ tens 9 ones

25. The mass of Mary's bag is about 3 _____ g/kg.

26. Subtract 73 from 100.

_____

27. **Draw the hands on the clock to show 9:10.**

Draw a part of a line, 4 inches long.

28.

Complete the number pattern.

29. 820, 840, 860, _____, _____, _____, 940

Draw what comes next.

30. ●▲○△●▲○△●▲○ ____

Look at the pattern. Check (✓) what comes next.

31.

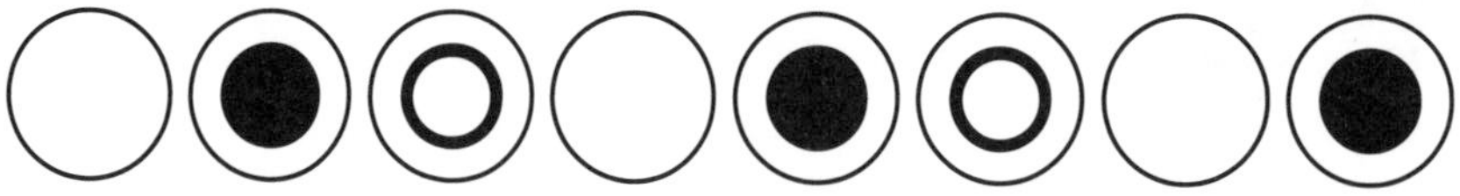

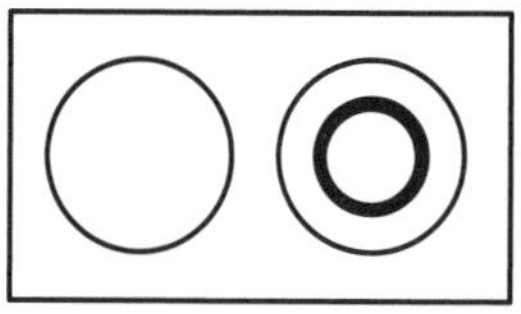

32.

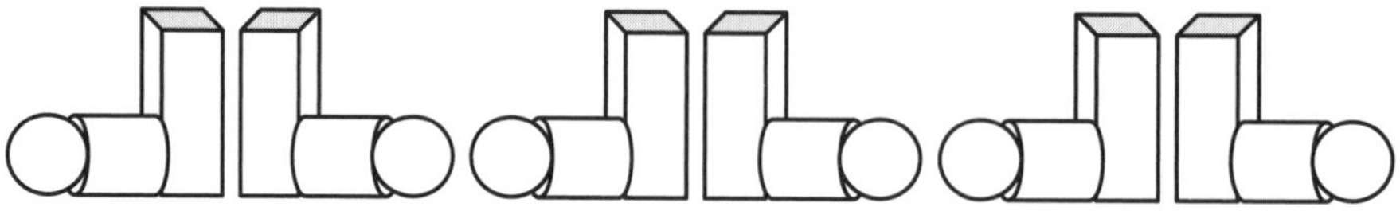

Name: ____________________ Date: ____________

Extended Response

The picture graph shows the number of storybooks each boy has.

Greg	○ ○ ○
Albert	○ ○ ○ ○
Mario	○ ○ ○ ○ ○
Anthony	○ ○
Each ○ stands for 3 books.	

Use the picture graph to fill in the blanks.

33. How many books does Greg have?

There are ____________ ○ for Greg.

____________ × ____________ = ____________

Greg has ____________ storybooks.

34. How many books do Albert and Anthony have in all?

There are _____ ◯ for Albert and Anthony.

_____ × _____ = _____

Albert and Anthony have _____ books in all.

35. How many storybooks does the boy with the greatest number of books have?

There are _____ ◯ for _____.

_____ × _____ = _____

He has _____ books in all.

36. How many more books does Mario have than Anthony?

Mario has 5 ◯.

_____ × _____ = _____

Anthony has _____ ◯.

_____ × _____ = _____

_____ – _____ = _____

Mario has _____ more books than Anthony.

Solve.
Show your work.

37.   Sam has 300 books.
He sells 118 books.
He lends 55 books to friends.
How many books does he have left?

He has _____ books left.

38.   Alexandra adds 200 grams of flour.
She adds 100 grams of butter.
She adds 150 grams of sugar.
Then she adds enough milk to make the total mass
1,000 grams.
How much milk does she add?

She adds _____ grams of milk.

Solve.
Show your work.
Use bar models to help you.

39. Abigail has $300. Mabel has $12 more than Abigail.

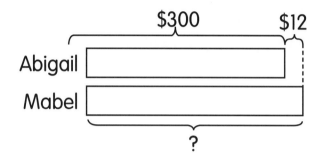

How much money does Mabel have?

Mabel has $_____.

40. 381 boys take part in a game.
78 fewer girls than boys take part in the game.

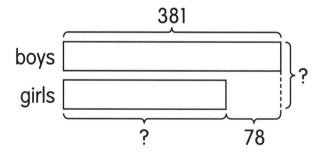

a. How many girls take part in the game?

_____ girls take part in the game.

b. How many children take part in the game?

_____ children take part in the game.